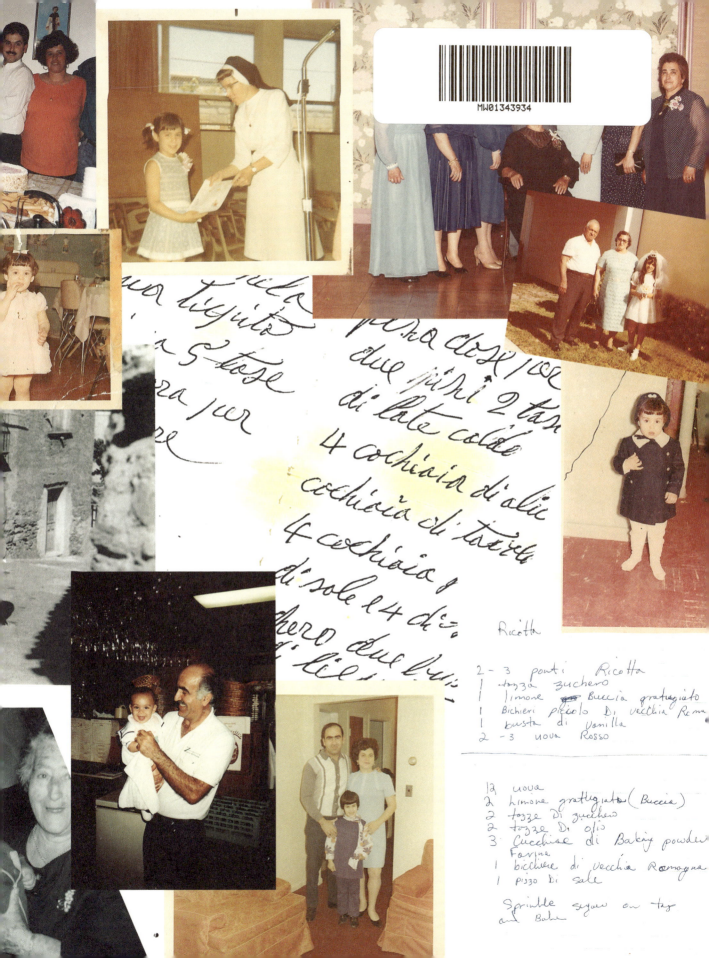

A CHAIR AT MY TABLE

Jennifer!
Let's Hot
Cooking
Abbracci!

OLIMPIA ZUCCARELLI

A CHAIR AT MY TABLE

BEING ZUCCARELLI: COOKING, EATING, LIVING

Copyright © 2014 by Olimpia Zuccarelli

All rights reserved. No part of this book may be used or reproduced in any manner whatsoever without prior written consent of the author, except as provided by the United States of America copyright law.

Published by Advantage, Charleston, South Carolina.
Member of Advantage Media Group.

ADVANTAGE is a registered trademark and the Advantage colophon is a trademark of Advantage Media Group, Inc.

Printed in the United States of America.

ISBN: 978-1-59932-492-0
LCCN: 2014953544

Book design by Megan Elger.

This publication is designed to provide accurate and authoritative information in regard to the subject matter covered. It is sold with the understanding that the publisher is not engaged in rendering legal, accounting, or other professional services. If legal advice or other expert assistance is required, the services of a competent professional person should be sought.

Advantage Media Group is proud to be a part of the Tree Neutral® program. Tree Neutral offsets the number of trees consumed in the production and printing of this book by taking proactive steps such as planting trees in direct proportion to the number of trees used to print books. To learn more about Tree Neutral, please visit **www.treeneutral.com**. To learn more about Advantage's commitment to being a responsible steward of the environment, please visit **www.advantagefamily.com/green**

Advantage Media Group is a publisher of business, self-improvement, and professional development books and online learning. We help entrepreneurs, business leaders, and professionals share their Stories, Passion, and Knowledge to help others Learn & Grow. Do you have a manuscript or book idea that you would like us to consider for publishing? Please visit **advantagefamily.com** or call **1.866.775.1696**.

A Chair at My Table is *dedicated to my mom, who taught me everything I know, and is my reason for writing this book.*

ACKNOWLEDGEMENTS

A Chair at My Table would not be possible without the loving support and guidance of several special people in my life.

First, I would like to thank my family, especially my mother, Frances, and my son, Michael. Without their guidance and unrelenting support, I would never have had the courage to write this book. Michael is my muse and inspires me to continue a family legacy. I am also grateful to all of my cousins, who listened to me and kept me grounded – you know who you are.

I would like to mention the wonderful and professional publishing team that has helped me make this book become a reality and dream come true. I would also like to recognize my creative photographer, Alfred, who miraculously captures the smells and taste of each of my recipes in a photograph.

Thank you to my friend, Anna Nicotra, for all of her encouragement and for supplying the props for many of my photo shoots. I would also like to acknowledge my ghostwriter, Elena Paynter, whose enthusiasm and unwavering faith in me has been a constant beacon of light during this incredible journey.

Finally, a big thank you to all of my great friends – without all of you, *A Chair at My Table* would have remained a dream.

INTRODUCTION 09
THE FAMILY BUSINESS

CHAPTER ONE 19
TIME TO MAKE THE SAUSAGE

CHAPTER TWO 27
IN THE KITCHEN WITH MOTHER, GRANDMOTHER, AND THE BEST INGREDIENTS

CHAPTER THREE 53
FAMILY DINNERS MADE WITH LOVE

CHAPTER FOUR 81
QUICK-AND-EASY WEEKDAY MEALS

CHAPTER FIVE 97
CLASSIC ZUCCARELLI RECIPES PAST AND PRESENT

CHAPTER SIX 131
HOLIDAYS AND SPECIAL OCCASIONS

CHAPTER SEVEN 157
SWEETS AND AFTER-DINNER TREATS

INTRODUCTION

THE FAMILY BUSINESS

It all started with my grandfather back in the little town of Mongrassano, located in the mountains of Calabria, a region of southern Italy on the toe of the boot, right next to Sicily. It was in the mountains of Calabria where my father was raised as a child. The first time I went there to visit my grandparents I was just five years old, and I remember how different Calabria was from where we were living in Westchester, New York. The town was very small, and the streets were so narrow that you'd be lucky to fit a car in their path. Consequently, most things were transported through town not by car, but in carts or on the backs of donkeys. There were a few streetlights, and the population was only about 1,500 people (which I think might have included all the chickens, pigs, horses, and donkeys in town).

I remember my grandmother taking me up a hill to a spring on the side of the mountain, where ice cold water spouted. It was here that she washed the clothes using an old washboard. When she finished, I'd help her carry the basket of clothes back home, and then I would ask, "Nana, what are we going to have for dinner tonight? She would reply, "Go in the backyard and pick what you want." In the backyard were chickens and rabbits, and I was confused, "What do you mean? I have to pick?" I was so young, I didn't understand. A little while later, I returned to the backyard and said, "Where are the chickens?" My grandmother said, "Well, they're on the table now."

My dad, who was the youngest of four brothers and four sisters, lived in a home above the family's café and delicatessen. In Italy, they call it a café, but it served more than just coffee; it was actually a local hangout where good food and liquor were served as well. The townspeople would gather there and sit outside at little tables to have an espresso and play Italian card games, and maybe listen to some music. Next door was the family's Old World Italian deli, or *salumeria*. Italian delis were a different story from what we think of today; they sold cheeses and Italian sausages, bread, olives, olive oil, anchovies, all kinds of food. Back then, they made everything from scratch—there was no such thing as packaged foods.

That's where my dad grew up, and that's where everything started. Then in 1954 he came to this country along with his brothers, and they started delis in Westchester County, New York, that were just like the delis they'd had back in Italy. They opened one deli in Yonkers and one in Mount Vernon, and from there the family grew.

My mother is also from Calabria, but from a town called Aprigliano Corte, a beautiful ski resort town. Her family had their own olive trees and, of course, a garden (both sides of the family had gardens, so there was very little need to go to the market). On the occasions when they did go to the market, it was to get a few staples, like sugar or a big burlap bag of dried beans that lasted forever and served as a base for inexpensive meals. Besides that, they raised, grew, or made all their own food. They made sausages and cheese, grew their own vegetables, jarred their own tomatoes, eggplants, and olives. My mom's family was really big on making their own desserts as well.

My mom came to the United States in 1955, when she was just 11 years old. One day she went to the movies in the Bronx with one of her girlfriends, who knew my dad and his family. When she and her girlfriend came out of the movie theater, they ran into my dad hanging around with his friends. At this point they turned around, went back into the theater, and saw the same movie again with the guys. Afterwards, my mom and dad got together and that was that.

Before my parents got engaged, my dad served in the military for about 18 months. After his tour of duty, they were married. I was born a year later, in 1965. My dad's parents' names were Mario and Olimpia. I carry my paternal grandmother's name because it is a tradition in Italy that the first son to have a daughter should name her after his mother.

In Mount Vernon, we lived in a three-family house with two of my uncles (my third uncle was off doing his own thing) and their families. Since my parents met, my mother has always worked full time, so in the early years my grandmother raised me with the help of my aunt downstairs. They looked after me while my mother was away working. I grew up with my three cousins—Mario, Fiore, and Joe. Although I'm an only child, they were like brothers to me and I was like the little sister they never had. I'm the youngest, but we are only a few years apart in age. Mario, the oldest, is seven years older than me, Fiore is five years older, and Joe is three years older. For a long time, I was the only girl in the family. Consequently, I was spoiled most of the time, until one of my uncles remarried and had two girls, and then my aunts had a couple of girls, too.

We lived on top of a hill on a one-way street, and my cousins used to build these go-karts out of scraps of things they would find in the trash or in people's yards. Because I was the youngest, they used me as the guinea pig. When there were no cars coming, they would put me in a go-kart and send me off down the hill to see if it worked. Of course, sometimes it would break down or the wheels would fall off, and I'd go flying and scrape up my knees.

Other than that, my cousins were very protective of me. I couldn't leave the house without them. If I was outside, they had to be outside too. And if another kid wanted to play with me, they had to be there too. We used to play hide and seek in the street with our neighbors' kids. We would play until the streetlights came on, and then my mother would open the window and call out to me, "You have to come inside," because I couldn't be outside after dark. I thought that was so embarrassing back then, but now I realize how nice it was that there were always lots of people looking out for me. I also think things were just simpler and safer then. We didn't even lock our doors at night, because we didn't feel like we had to. I don't know anyone who has that peace of mind anymore.

It's just amazing how close we all were. I was never alone. I never felt like an only child because there was family always around me. Whenever we took a family vacation, my mom would ask one of my cousins to come along to keep me company. As children, my youngest cousin Joe and I had the same voice and sometimes our mothers couldn't tell us apart when they heard one of us calling out. When I would call out for my mom in the middle of the night, my aunt would always go to Joe's room and check on him, and he was always asleep. The same would happen when Joe called out for his mom—my mom would come to my room and check up on me and find me sleeping soundly. To this day, my cousins and I still talk about the old days growing up and how we were always together.

Italian is our first language. The entire family spoke Italian to each other. When I started kindergarten, I spoke very little English. By the time I went to Catholic school, the nuns said, "Listen, you take care of the Italian at home, and we'll handle the English at school." Eventually I learned to speak English in school, but we always spoke Italian at home. I've always been fluent in Italian. I can read it and write it, and I even translate from it. Knowing the language helps me run the restaurant, because I can do business with Italian purveyors here at home, and abroad when I am in Italy. Even though they know I'm American, they say, "My God, you speak so well for someone living in the United States."

In 1971, my dad's oldest brother, Uncle Fiore, wasn't feeling well, so he decided to take a trip to Florida for the warm climate. His plan was just to visit a friend and take it easy for a little bit, but he fell in love with Florida. He spent some time scouting out the area with his real-estate friend, and he realized, "Wow, what we do would be perfect down here, because there's nothing, no real Italian food down here at all."

Next thing you know, he approached my other uncle and my dad and said, "I think we should open up a deli like we have now, but down in Florida. I think it could work." He had found a location in Pompano Beach, and wanted my father and uncles to come down and check it out. It was close to Fort Lauderdale, about forty-five minutes from Miami Beach, and there were practically no delis or cafes around it at the time—just some supermarkets and little else. My uncle Fiore was the oldest brother, and he was a natural businessman. He really felt that this was a good opportunity to grow our business and our family, and he was right. Besides, he didn't want to leave Florida and go back to New York.

Sadly for me, my cousins Mario, Fiore, and Joe didn't want to leave their friends in New York, and my uncle Vinnie still had the deli to run in Mount Vernon, so none of them wanted to move. (In fact, they're still there today, and so is the deli.) But my dad said, "Well, then we'll go." I was eight years old when my mom, dad, and I moved to Florida with my uncle Fiore to start a deli business in Pompano. Once a month, we would receive a trailer load filled with Italian specialties from a Brooklyn company–the best Italian purveyor around! And just like his family used to do in Calabria, my father would make his own mozzarella and sausage, and that's how we introduced our concept to South Florida.

My uncle Fiore became my mentor. He, along with my mother and father, taught me everything I know today about running a business. They all had strong work ethics and were great teachers. Of course, when I was young I thought they were mean and nasty when they made me work, but now I understand why. I owe my success to all of those lessons they taught me since I was a little girl, and with the help of my mother.

Little by little, my dad's sisters followed us down to Florida, later followed by my other uncle, Silvio. Later, my grandmother Olimpia came down when my aunt Rose moved to Florida. At the time, my grandparents had been going back and forth to Italy. My grandfather wanted to move back to Italy because that's where his heart was, but my grandmother wanted to stay in the States, where all her children and grandchildren were growing up. My grandfather had been helping out with the business when he was around, but when he got older, he stepped down and my father and uncles took over the business.

Over the years, we steadily built up our reputation. We did very little advertising—it was all word of mouth. There wasn't much of an Italian community in Pompano at the time, but people came and they liked the food. It was as if the market had been calling for something that we alone could offer. Back then, there were no other businesses like it. So the deli began to grow a little bit at a time, and then it got busier and busier. That's how everything started, over 40 years ago, in Pompano, South Florida.

People today still talk about the old deli. They'll come into our current place and say something like, "Oh, was your family the one that had the deli down in Pompano? That was the best thing. I still remember going there as a child." After eight years there, my father and my uncle wanted to do something else, so we divided the building in half; we kept the deli on one side and started a pizzeria on the other, and this created the restaurant.

At the deli—we called it Zuccarelli's Delicatessen—you could buy olives, olive oils, wine, tons of different kinds of pasta, and breads that we got delivered fresh every day. In addition to serving lots and lots of sandwiches, we also served our homemade mozzarella, which was our claim to fame. (People would come in just for that!) Then, at the pizzeria, we offered sit-down dining, take-out, or delivery. We would open the deli at 7:00 a.m., and then at 6:00 p.m. we would close the deli by closing the divider between the deli and the pizzeria. We would walk around to the pizzeria through the kitchen. The pizzeria would remain open until midnight. My father made the pizza so he worked a lot of hours, and so did my mother. As for me, I just had to help out for a little bit and then go home to get ready for school the next day. However, once I graduated, I worked in the restaurant full time.

We made Neapolitan-style pizza—some people here call it New York-style—which is thin and round. We also made Sicilian-style pizza, which is square and thick. We made our own dough, which was very light. People used to say, "Oh, that looks heavy," and I would have to explain to them, "No, it's not. It's very light. It's just a different style."

The pizzeria was a hit, and after a while we started adding dishes, one at a time. That's when my mother really started creating new dishes and adding them to the menu. The menu has expanded through the years, but has remained the same in a way. It has always been based on the same Old World recipes my mother grew up with, the same authentic ingredients, and the same history which is behind everything.

In time, the business was getting to be a lot of work, and everybody wanted to go their own way and try something new. In 1981, we sold the deli and pizzeria, and my parents and I went into the restaurant business in nearby Margate. The new restaurant was solely run by my parents and me. My uncle Fiore opened his own restaurant in West Palm Beach and was successful there until he passed away suddenly in 1982. Consequently, my aunt wanted to move back to Italy with her children, so we sold our restaurant in

Margate and bought my uncle Fiore's restaurant in West Palm Beach from her. We've been there now for more than 30 years.

My mother is still here in the kitchen every day, my father comes in periodically to make sausage and a few other things, and, of course, I'm now here full time. We have employees who have been with us for decades, some for more than 20 years. We don't have a big turnover like most restaurants do, because we're a team. There is nothing I wouldn't ask them to do that I wouldn't do myself. I'm at the restaurant seventy to eighty hours a week, so I think of it as my house. It's my house and the people who come here are my guests. They're my family and close friends who I have known forever.

When my son, Michael, was born 23 years ago, I was a single mother, so I used to take a porta-crib to the restaurant and put it behind the bar so he could sleep and still be near me and my mother.

OLIMPIA ZUCCARELLI | 15

All the customers would want to play with him, but he mostly slept through all the noise and activity. I was lucky to have such a good baby. Just like me, Michael grew up in the business. Because I wanted Michael to have a childhood and be able to be a little boy and not miss out on things, I made sure that he was always very busy with school activities and sports. Although he has worked a lot at the restaurant, he has chosen his own path and decided to follow a career in law enforcement. I'm really glad that I've been able to give him the family environment that we've built, both at home and at the restaurant. Times have changed and he's doing his own thing, but I'm still glad that I've been able to pass on our family history and values to my son.

At the restaurant, we've developed some great relationships over the years, and so many people have watched my son grow up. Quite a few of them have been coming here for so long that they even have watched me grow up. People still come in who used to go to our place in Pompano, and they'll say, "Don't tell me you're that same little girl who used to be there all the time." It's like we've all grown up together.

I have people who have been coming here since day one, which means they have been eating at our place for more than 30 years. When you've been in business 30 years, you see people grow and change. I've watched people come in with their parents, then with their friends and significant others, then with their spouses, and now with their own kids. In fact, I have a couple *hundred* customers today who have been coming since day one. They still remember all sorts of things about the old days—even some things I don't remember myself—like the wooden salad bowls we first used, the carafes of wine we used to put on the tables, and the paper napkins we used when we were just starting out. They remember our old booths, which were red, white, and green, the colors of the Italian flag.

I almost cringe when I think about some of those things, but then I think I can't knock them because they made us what we are today. We were the only restaurant in the area at that time, tucked

ZUCCARELLI'S NORTH

Practically my whole extended family went into the food business. There's still a deli called Zuccarelli's in Eastchester, New York, near the house where I first lived in Westchester before we moved to Florida. It's still run by my uncle Vinny and my cousins Fiore, Joe, and Mario, who were like older brothers to me when we were young and living in the same house. When I was in high school, I went back there for a year so I could graduate with my friends. The high school was down the street from their deli, so I used to occasionally work with them. They've been in the same spot now for nearly 40 years, making and selling all the great, Old World food, like sausages and homemade mozzarella, which my grandparents used to make at their own deli back in Italy.

away in a corner, and we built our reputation from nothing, through word of mouth, to the thriving establishment we have today. The restaurant is so different now in how looks and how we run it, but the memories are still there, and so are the authentic recipes and the Old World values. When I look back, I wouldn't change a thing about how we got here.

We've been lucky to have a lot of loyal customers over the years. Our customers are really what have made our success. I wouldn't be here today without them. Yes, we have great family values, and great food and atmosphere, but our customers found us, and their loyalty has helped make us what we are today. Making all these people happy has been one of the best, most satisfying parts of my life; that's why I wanted to write this book. I want to share with everyone my experiences, my upbringing, my family, and our way of cooking, eating, and living. In my family, we've all worked so hard all our lives, but I really believe we know how to live well. I want people to see that the Old World still exists and that the old way of doing things still has a real place in this world.

CHAPTER ONE

TIME TO MAKE THE SAUSAGE!

I love to reminisce about my childhood visits to my father's hometown of Mongrassano in Calabria, Italy. The town was so quaint, doors and windows always open because there was no such thing as air conditioning. Summer days were warm, and the evenings would welcome the cool mountain breezes. It wasn't too often that Mongrassano had the chance to welcome American visitors. Through the eyes of a child, it was as though the whole town knew we were coming to visit, and when we arrived it felt like a celebration—everyone was so excited to see us! Everyone in town thought I was born in Italy, because I spoke Italian, not English. Although my parents spoke English, they only spoke Italian to me. A favorite pastime in Mongrassano was taking an evening stroll around the middle of the town square (a *piazza* in Italian) and stopping occasionally to have a conversation or two with anyone who wanted to chat. Sometimes there was an event in the piazza and the festivities would last until early in the morning. It was a lot of fun. Life in Mongrassano was at a much slower pace than my home in New York!

Back in New York, my father worked every day at our deli, just like he had done as a young man growing up in Italy. Every morning, I'd get ready for school and meet my cousins Fiore, Joe, and Mario in front of the deli, and we would all pile into the deli's powder blue van and wait for my father or my uncle to drive us to school. Afterward, my father would go straight back to the deli, open up, and start making the food. After school, my cousins and I would all meet outside the school building, and we'd walk together to the deli and help out for a while before going home. That's how I first started to learn how to prepare Italian food.

Everybody thinks Italians are loud and crazy, but not my family. My father is a quiet and kind person. It was always very quiet in the kitchen when he and I were there together. He gets very focused in what he does and he loves it. My father taught me that you have to love what you do in this business, because it's so much work and it takes so much time and effort. At 73, he is still working, though not as much as he used to, and he's still doing everything the old-fashioned way. My father has never used a measuring cup or a scale to measure ingredients; because he's been doing it for so long, he is comfortable measuring ingredients by eye and by feel.

While I was growing up, my father taught me about making sausage by teaching me easy tasks like washing the casings for the sausages and the basic technique of how to roll up cold cuts for the antipasto platters, both of which felt like they took forever to finish. After I finished washing the casings, my father would let me help him make the sausage by turning the handle on our old-fashioned sausage maker, which forced the meat into the sausage casings. I would be turning it and turning it while my father would be saying, "Stop, go, stop, go, wait, it's breaking! OK go."

As a child, I was able to crank the handle of the sausage maker to stuff all types of sausages except for the sausage mix that had cheese in it. We used (and still use) hard Romano cheese, which means you have to turn the crank really hard to force the sausage through the machine. Eventually, I got older and stronger and was able to handle the cheese sausages too! My father also taught me how to twist and roll the sausages and put them into a pan to store in the refrigerator, and how to cut and weigh the sausage. It was during that quality time together with my father that I started to learn the fundamentals about how to prepare Italian food correctly.

Another lesson I learned was the importance of a clean kitchen. All of my family members stressed the importance of a clean kitchen, but especially my *nonno* (grandfather) Mario, my dad's father. As is our family tradition, my cousin Mario is the first-born grandson and was named after *Nonno* Mario just like I was named after my grandmother Olimpia. My grandfather Mario always wore an apron and had a towel sticking out of his back pocket. He would tell me that I should keep a towel—a *straccio* as he called it—on me at all times to use for cleaning, since there is always something to clean in a kitchen. When I was very young, he would lift me up and sit me on the shelves where the cans of food and bottles of olive oil were stored. My task was to clean each can and bottle, one by one, and place each one back on the shelf, making sure they were all lined up straight with every product label facing outward before I was done. The rule was that if I didn't clean each can or bottle properly or left some dust on the shelf, I would have to do it all over again.. Today, Zuccarelli's restaurant has an open kitchen that faces our customers, because I want our customers to see the superior level of cleanliness we strive to maintain in our kitchen. Our pots and pans are immaculate! I'm sure my instinct to set up the kitchen this way stems from those early lessons that were drilled into me as a child about the crucial importance of cleanliness.

Because I was the lucky one to share my father's mother's name, Olimpia, I was always a little bit spoiled by her. It's funny to me now, when I remember how she would sneak money into my hands and say, "Shh, don't tell your father." Because I was a girl and an only child, I was always well supervised and rarely left alone, and some people thought I was spoiled. I never really understood why, considering how much work I did growing up. Obviously those people never saw me sitting on the shelves dusting cans or at the counter for hours rolling up cold cuts. My father, grandfather, and uncles gave all of their children great work ethics. From the time that I was small enough to fit on those kitchen shelves, they were always teaching us that hard work is the recipe for success!

Eventually, I grew tall enough to reach the counter and was able to learn a whole bunch of new skills. I went from easier tasks like dusting shelves and turning the sausage crank to harder ones like cutting forms of cheese and cleaning the slicing machines. When I was just 10 years old, I was taught how to clean the slicers without getting cut!

I spent my afternoons finishing my homework on the deli counter and then rolling the cold cuts and cleaning up. Although I was much younger than any of the employees, I was taught to be a leader and always set an example. Leading by example meant wearing what we called our "uniform," which in our kitchen meant you always had to have an apron on, your hair pulled back, closed shoes, no jewelry, and an overall clean appearance. I learned how to operate a restaurant from the bottom up. When I was 13 and we had our place in Margate, I started waiting tables. My dad was in charge of making pizza, and my mom was cooking all the other dishes. At the time, we had a waitress named Deborah who showed me how to be a good waitress. She was only in her twenties and a hard worker. She taught me all the fundamentals of how to serve, from A to Z, including serving etiquette like how to speak to people at the tables, how to carry a tray full of dishes, how to place things on the table without reaching over people, and so on. Waitressing was a whole new world for me. Deborah ended up staying with us for more than 15 years, until she moved away with her family. Thanks to Deborah, I started making $90 a night! For someone who was barely a teenager, that was pretty good money! Sometimes I would work the door and occasionally still do. I also worked in the kitchen by making certain specialties or just helping out. At some point in my life, I've worked every job there is in the restaurant, so I can always say I'm a hands-on owner!

I learned how to make everything from scratch. Eventually we bought our own pasta machines and started making homemade pasta. We made (and still make) our own tortellini, manicotti, ravioli, linguini, fettuccini, spaghetti, all sorts of shaped pastas, even macaroni! We made gnocchi too. I'd put the pasta in baggies, weigh and label the bags of pasta, and store them in the freezer to keep them fresh. Today, we are continuing the family's traditional methods that my father learned in my grandfather's deli in Italy. We have never changed. I've made improvements in terms of running the business end of the restaurant, but the quality of the food, the labor, and the preparation have always been done the old-fashioned way. And we still speak Italian in the kitchen! My mother picks fresh vegetables daily and cooks every meal to order, even our salads! Our customers

GNOCCHI
Pasta made from potatoes.

don't mind waiting for food, because they know we don't have pre-prepared dishes. The quality and presentation of our food is very important to us.

It's hard work running a restaurant the way we do because it's very labor intensive. We are lucky to have a team in the kitchen that's been with us a long time; that's what separates us from other restaurants. It is rare to find a restaurant like Zuccarelli's that continues to use an Old World cooking approach when creating new recipes.

SAUSAGE

Most restaurants buy already prepared sausages. At Zuccarelli's we take pride in continuing to use traditional methods when preparing our unique sausage recipes. We make three kinds of sausage: 1) hot sausage with a little bit of red pepper and paprika; 2) sweet sausage with little pieces of fennel; and 3) a skinny sausage called *cervellata* made with Romano cheese and parsley. We still use an old-fashioned sausage machine with a crank! The machine is at least 20 years old. Electric sausage machines are available so that you don't have to crank the handle by hand, but we prefer the old sausage machine because we like to be in full control of how the meat fills the sausage casings.

One secret to making good sausage is using only the finest ingredients. The most important secret, though, is trimming the pork butts clean by cutting out a lot of the fat. Getting rid of the excess fat keeps the sausage from shrinking as you cook it, because the fat cooks off. Once the sausage is cooked, it remains intact. Our sausage recipes are so popular that we sell up to 500 pounds of sausage every 2 weeks. High season begins right before the beginning of winter. This is when "snowbirds" fly down to Florida to escape the bitter cold. During high season, demand for our homemade sausages increases and we have to produce at least twice as much sausage! We also increase production during the holiday season, because people come in and ask to buy the sausages to take some home. Although we are no longer a deli, customers still come in and say, "I can't find good sausage anywhere. Can I buy some of yours?" And I say, "Of course! Everything's for sale here!" People buy it by the pound and put it on the grill at home.

We grind the meat ourselves and then mix the ground meat with herbs and other ingredients before we put it in the sausage maker. The casings have to be washed one at a time under the faucet. We use lambskin casings packed in salt, so we have to wash them off thoroughly so we don't get salty sausage. The sausage casing goes around the tube on the sausage maker where the meat comes out. The casing has to be held tight so that the meat completely fills the casing, until the sausage is firm and without any air pockets (air pockets will make the sausage become all soft and mushy). We carefully pack the meat in the casing as tightly as we can, and that's how we end up with some of the best sausage around!

MOZZARELLA

One of our first house specialties was our homemade mozzarella. People would come to the deli from all around town just for our fresh mozzarella. Every morning when I was young, I would watch my father make fresh mozzarella. When it was nearly done and all nice and smooth and oozing down, I loved to rip off a piece, put a little salt on it, and pop it in my mouth when it was still warm and gooey. Fresh and hot mozzarella is one of my favorite things!

Homemade mozzarella is not hard to make, but it does take a few hours. The mozzarella has to sit in hot water and be stirred periodically. When you lift it up with a pallet and it's all gooey and hot, that's when it's ready to eat! I'd watch my dad cut it, roll it, and shape it into the little purses. Or he'd flatten the mozzarella on a table, and layer it with thin-sliced prosciutto to make *mozzarella con prosciutto*. Then we'd roll it, tie it with a rope, and put it in the refrigerator. We'd cut the mozzarella and sell it by the pound.

Sometimes we would take half of the batch of our fresh mozzarella and smoke it. We would let the mozzarella dry out in the

CUSTOMER STORY

We've had one great customer for over 40 years! He used to come to our deli in Pompano with his mom and two brothers. He watched me grow up and still remembers me as a little kid. He remembers how crowded the deli used to be, and that despite how busy my dad was in taking orders and making sandwiches, as soon as my father or one of my uncles saw him, they'd stop what they were doing and quickly make him a little sandwich so he could go sit at a table away from the crowd and enjoy his meal.

refrigerator, then tie a rope around it and hang it in a big can with a piece of smoking wood at the bottom, and cover the whole thing with a towel or an apron. The smoke gets into the cheese and turns it from a pale white to a mild golden color. My father would let me sit and watch over the mozzarella as it smoked. When the mozzarella was the the right color, I would take all the mozzarella out and my father would come and put out the fire.

Smoked mozzarella is really good melted on a piece of bread. I love cheese—if you didn't know any better, you'd think I was a mouse!

CHAPTER TWO

IN THE KITCHEN WITH MOTHER, GRANDMOTHER, AND THE BEST INGREDIENTS

My mother's parents, Marietta and Giovanni Costanzo, grew up in a small town in Calabria, Italy, called Aprigliano Corte. My grandmother was very proud of her *il giardino*, which is Italian for garden. She grew an Italian garden that, depending on the season, would include tomatoes, zucchini, sweet peppers, hot peppers, cucumbers, onions, squash, and fig trees, and she even grew grapes on a grapevine on the terrace. She especially loved growing squash because of the blossoms, which are considered a delicacy in Italy. My grandfather and grandmother planted everything themselves, and they were excellent gardeners.

After my grandparents emigrated from Italy to the United States, my grandmother continued the tradition by growing another Italian garden behind their house in Tuckahoe, New York. Because my mother was working full time at the family delicatessen in Mount Vernon, she would drop me off at my grandmother's house so that my grandmother, Marietta, and my *zia* (aunt) Nella could help care for me. I remember summertime in Tuckahoe and how funny the zucchinis grew. They were so big they looked like hanging baseball bats! At my grandmother's house, life seemed to revolve around what we were going to prepare for dinner that evening. I loved to watch my grandmother fuss and prepare the evening's meal. She was an amazing cook—and an awesome grandmother!

My grandmother would spend the day making all sorts of Italian goodies, such as cheese, sausage, jarred tomatoes, and tomato sauce. My grandfather even made homemade red wine down in the basement, crushing the grapes himself with his wine press. My grandparents used that same wine press to make preserved olives, as well. My uncles and grandfather would buy seventy or eighty cases of green olives from a supplier in the Bronx. I remember how the whole family would sit on the terrace under the grapevines, using bricks to crack the olives and remove the pits so the olives could go into the press. Pressing the olives was a family event! I have fond memories of everyone holding bricks, cracking the olives, and drinking homemade wine while watching the Ziploc bags my grandmother washed and hung on the laundry line swaying back and forth, till they were completely dry. My grandmother loved to recycle! My family would add water or ice to the wine to dilute it so I could have a little bit, too! Sometimes my grandfather would even put a little Coca-Cola in with it. So everyone would be drinking homemade red wine, talking, laughing, and saying, "Come on, get to work!" or "*Adiamos a lavorare*!" in Italian. There was no sitting around and watching TV when there was so much work to be done! I still have that wine press. In honor of my grandfather, I had it restored and now it is on display in my restaurant.

The wine press squeezes out all the oils from the olives, which makes the olives shrink and become wrinkly. My grandparents would take the wrinkled olives and pack them tightly in mason jars, and cover them in olive oil with a little bit of celery, red pepper, and fennel. They would boil the filled mason jars in hot water until the jars were sealed tight. My mother continues to make olives this way in the restaurant, where she will offer our customers a sample or include them on an appetizer plate.

Whatever my grandmother couldn't grow in the garden or make in the kitchen, she would have my grandfather buy at the grocery store. My grandfather, Giovanni, was the head of the household and was responsible for the family's finances. Going to the store was an event for my grandfather. I remember how he would dress up in a suit and a hat and then call my mother so she could drive him to the store. Out of eight siblings (six sisters and two brothers), my mother and her brother were the only ones who learned how to drive a car. To this day, none of my mother's sisters know how to drive. My grandfather would have my mother drive an extra mile out of the way to save a dollar on a bottle of olive oil. He never calculated the extra cost in gasoline or the time it took to drive farther away to save a dollar. My grandfather was funny that way. Making a deposit at

SQUASH BLOSSOMS

My grandmother Marietta passed her love for squash blossoms to my mother. The edible, yellow-orange flowers of the squash or zucchini are a delicacy that my mother loves. They're seasonal and only available in the summertime, which makes the flowers hard to find.

My mother prepares the squash blossoms by washing them lightly, coating them in flour and egg batter, and then pan frying them for a little bit. Add a little salt, and you can serve them cold or hot, just like that. People ask for them at the restaurant all the time, so once in a while, my zio (uncle) Luigi, who lives in New York, vacuum-packs the blossoms for us and sends them to my mom, which makes her very happy. Unfortunately, I never developed a taste for squash flowers. I guess I didn't "feel the love"!

the bank was also a special occasion. I'll never forget how, when my grandfather had to go to the bank, he would dress up in his finest suit and fedora hat! It was such a big deal to him. He had all his money for the deposit rolled up and wrapped with a rubber band around it. My grandfather was a sharp as a tack, and he knew where every dollar was spent in the household. He always balanced his account to the penny!

I remember my grandmother always asking me to go out and grab fresh vegetables in the garden for her, and then I'd help her prepare them in the kitchen. She was always instructing me, "You need to do this, you need to do that." She'd have me wash all the vegetables, and then I'd begin peeling the skins off and she'd stop me and say, "No, the skin is good! It's got all the vitamins in there." Just like my grandmother, my mother is very particular about selecting the best quality and freshness of the ingredients she uses to make food.

My grandmother was raised with Old World values. She was hard working and preferred doing everything the old-fashioned way. I can still hear my grandmother each time my mother says, "Don't waste anything," "Save your money," and "Don't be too trusting." I was taught to respect my elders, so as I was growing up, I would call any adult "Aunt" or "Uncle" as a sign of respect. My family had the original open-door policy. Our door was always open and anyone was welcomed at our house. Just walk in, pull out a chair at the table, and enjoy the food and company. No invitation needed!

Although I spent a lot of time working and helping my family with the family business, my mother never lost sight of maintaining a balance in my life. She always made sure to preserve my childhood by enrolling me in fun activities, like joining the Brownies and taking ballet classes. My mother is amazing. Despite her full schedule between the family business and her daily responsibilities at home, she managed to find the time to share with me. My mother always made sure I had time to play and make friends.

When I was a teenager, I looked forward to going out with my girlfriends and dancing. My girlfriends would always stop by and pick me up to go dancing after I finished my shift at the restaurant. Sometimes, if we weren't too busy, my mom would let me leave a little early. My mom is so sweet. After dancing, we were always hungry, but instead of going to diners like most of the kids our age, I used to bring along pizza or calzones from the restaurant and keep them in the trunk of the car. So after we left the clubs, we'd go hang out in the parking lot and eat pizza. My family believed in no work, no play.

When I turned eight years old, and moved to Florida, my mom's entire family remained in New York. My mother wasn't happy about leaving them behind, but the opportunity in Florida was too great to pass up. Her parents would come to Florida and visit, but they never could get used to the climate and the unfamiliar environment. I guess the older they grew the more set in their ways they became, and the idea of making a change was uncomfortable.

After the move to Florida, my family was split geographically, and my mother and I became a team. My mother instilled in me the foundation of my work ethic. She is a true reflection of my grandmother. She has a full heart and is very kind and thoughtful. She is also a bottomless font of wisdom and continues to be an unlimited source of great advice and guidance. When people are thoughtless or mean to me, my mother always advises, "Just keep your chin up and keep going. Rise above them. Let people talk. It's okay. Don't answer them. Don't ever come down to their level. You just have to understand where it's coming from, and keep going, because you know who you are." I am thankful for my mother's advice every day, because she has kept me focused on the positive and helped me build character and strength.

CHOOSING TO SERVE

Being a single mother and raising a son is not easy. I couldn't tell you which was harder: Raising my son or running a restaurant. Regardless, I managed to do both at the same time! Every day, I strive to pass

ZUCCARELLI FAMILY VALUES

My family believes in Old World food and Old World values. My dad would always open doors for women: car doors, front doors, any door. He believes that ladies should enter first. In my family, women and men had traditional roles. Women were responsible for running the household and men were responsible for the family's finances. My father, like my grandfather, paid all of the bills. After dinners together, the family would split up. The women and children would clean the dirty dishes and the dining room, while the men would socialize and smoke in the living room. There was no sitting down and relaxing for me, my mom, or my aunts until everything was completely cleaned, washed, and put away. If for any reason I didn't feel like helping or showed disrespect, my mother would show me who was in charge by lightly swatting my behind with a wooden spoon. It didn't take too many swats to convince me who was the boss!

ALWAYS THE OLD-SCHOOL WAY

For over 30 years, the restaurant used one of those old manual cash registers. Even though I now use computers to operate and manage the restaurant, my mother still likes using that old manual cash register. When she's ringing up a takeout order, which she does often from the kitchen counter, she uses that same old cash register! She says, "That's just what I like. I like to be control in what I'm doing, and I don't like to push the buttons on these new machines." My mother is definitely old school!

on my family's most cherished traditions to my son, Michael. I want to instill in him the importance of family values. In spite of all the negative pressures placed on young people in a modern world, Michael has steadfastly remained on the right track in life. I am very proud of my son. When Michael was a baby, I didn't want a stranger watching Michael in my home. My parents had recently moved into a new house and my mother didn't want me to raise Michael on my own, so I moved in with my parents to give Michael a family environment. Michael became the son my parents never had. He grew up in the family business and, like me, had different chores to do as he grew older. Unfortunately, my parents divorced, and my mother, Michael, and I remain living together at home and working together at the restaurant.

My mother always told me I should finish high school and go to college to get an education. She wanted me to explore, to see if there was something else I wanted to do with my life. She knew that the restaurant business is hard work and that you have to dedicate yourself to the success of the restaurant. She knew that operating a successful restaurant would require long hours and few days off. I attended the Broward School of Court Reporting, finished my courses, and became a stenographer. But I came to realize that managing and operating the restaurant was in my blood and that cooking is my passion. I truly believe this is my calling in life. I love attending to the needs of my customers. I love the hustle and bustle of a busy day at the restaurant, and mostly, I love to cook! It is a challenge to reinvent and maintain a modern kitchen in an Old World environment! But I love that part too.

As our customer base grew, demands for a larger selection of dishes increased. My mother and I began creating new and exciting dishes, which we offered our customers and added to the menu. The menu grew rather large. It seemed that the larger the menu grew, the larger our customer base grew. And as our customer base grew, our kitchen requirements grew. The kitchen started with eight burners to cook on, then twelve burners, and now we're up to forty burners! So we had to hire cooks, too. One thing led to another and my mother eventually had to begin to delegate responsibilities to the kitchen staff. It was just too much work for her. So we evolved from just mom and dad in the kitchen with me helping out, to having five chefs cooking dishes, a pizza guy, and two prep guys in the kitchen, to cut and pound the chicken and veal, and make fresh sausage, meatballs, eggplant, pizza dough, sauces, and soups. Since we practically make everything by hand on the premises, there's a whole lot of work to do!

THE BEST INGREDIENTS

My mother's formal name is Franca, but she prefers to be called Frances. Some of my friends and customers love her so much they call her Mom. She doesn't mind. My mother is the star attraction of the restaurant. When customers come in, they always ask for her. If she's not in the restaurant, they'll often become upset. They'll keep asking, "Where is she? Where'd she go?" She's as much of a draw to many of our customers as the food!

My mother is the backbone of the business, and she creates dishes by simply testing them to see how they work and how they taste. Her southern Italian style of cooking is simple, not fancy, but because of that, she insists on the best and freshest ingredients. And wherever she can, she makes the basics herself, like roasted red peppers. We still roast the peppers ourselves in our pizza oven, and peel them one at a time, and then my mother marinates them. They taste so much better than the jarred ones you find in the grocery store, it's almost like they were made from different ingredients!

I'm a volume restaurant, and I don't believe in gouging people or charging so much that it takes them another month or two before they can afford to come back. I'd rather charge a little less for good food and have my customers visit more often. Being sensitive to my customer's needs creates word-of-mouth recommendations and it's a win–win situation!

FRANCES ON HER CHILDHOOD ON AN ITALIAN FARM

"I was born and raised on a farm. I grew up in the fields with my sisters and parents. My father didn't go to an office to work. He cultivated the land, not to sell the food, but so he could raise his family. The only things my mom and my dad bought were salt and sugar. We even grew our own wheat, which my dad would take to the local mill to get made into flour for the bread that we baked. In other words, we ate all organic food.

"We kept animals like chickens, goats, lamb, and rabbits. We also had horses and donkeys that we used for travel, because we lived almost an hour from the city. In order for us to go to the little city where the shops were, we had to hop on a horse or a donkey.

"My parents worked very hard, but they didn't have the stress people have today. People today are not happy with what they've got. If they have a Toyota, they want a Cadillac. If they have a Cadillac, they want a Mercedes.

We didn't have anything, but we had everything. We were happy. Today, people have everything, but they don't really have anything.

"It was really primitive where we lived. There was no electricity. We used oil lamps at night. But it was a fun way to grow up. My mom used to send us younger ones into the field with just a piece of bread. We'd climb the trees and get figs or pick a tomato, wipe it off on our clothes, and eat it with our bread. It was simple stuff, but it was really the best. My toys were baby chicks and a ragdoll that my mom made for me, and that's it. No bicycle. No video games. None of these computers and stuff.

"I wouldn't trade my childhood with the richest kid today. We were six sisters, two brothers, and my mom and my sisters and I all cooked. Then I came to the United States and we made our own thing. But I always remember how we did things on the farm. That's why I am very fussy about what I buy today."

This philosophy means spending a little more money for better-quality meat and produce. In the end, you don't end up paying that much more to prepare great food, and the payoff is always having a satisfied customer!

At 70 years old, my mother still goes to the vegetable market herself and picks out the produce we use every day, to make sure everything is perfectly ripe and fresh. People always ask us about our produce—where do we get it, why is it so good? I always say, my mother's eye is the judge. She grew up on a farm in Italy, so she knows what to look for. She knows what's best. If what she finds at the market isn't in tip-top shape, then she just won't buy it. We simply won't serve a certain dish that day rather than serve something made from mediocre ingredients.

HERE IS SOME OF OUR ADVICE ON HOW TO CHOOSE THE BEST INGREDIENTS:

TOMATOES

My mother is particularly picky about her tomatoes. They have to be red and ripe. The type of tomato you choose is not nearly as important as its freshness. We buy the freshest tomatoes available at the store that day. It could be Roma tomatoes or regular tomatoes or something else. It's the quality of the tomatoes that matters most, not the size or kind. They just have to be ripe and red and firm, so you get that really nice tomato taste.

SEAFOOD

We ensure our seafood is fresh by getting daily deliveries and buying only small quantities. The fish guy always says, "Why don't you buy a little bit more, and just keep it in the back?" We always say, "No, I want it fresh every day." Sometimes we sell out of something by 8 p.m. or 9 p.m., but we think that's better than ordering big quantities and using it for a few days in a row. We want it fresh! fresh! fresh!

For example, *scungilli* is a specialty item made with conch, and is hard to get. We've been buying a certain product since my father started this business. Now we use the same product for the scungilli we have on the menu. We won't change. We've been buying the same product most of our lives. One time I ordered it, and they didn't have the brand I wanted, so they sent me another one. I called them up and said, "What are you doing? This is not what I use." They said, "Well, we're out of stock on the other." I said, "Well then don't send me anything. I'd rather tell the customer it's out of stock than give them something that's not as good."

Some basic tips when you're looking for quality seafood are to look at it closely, poke it for texture (it should be firm), smell it (there should be no smell at all), and feel it (it should be sort of dry). When refrigerating fish, we recommend wrapping it in plastic so it stays dry (water should not touch the fish), and then storing it with a bag of ice so it stays extra cold.

PASTA

Unless you are ready to make your own pasta by hand, your best option would be to buy a store-packaged pasta from your local grocery store. Choose an Italian brand name that is made with 100 percent semolina, and always follow the cooking directions on the package for the best result!

OLIVE OIL

Zuccarelli's always uses extra-virgin olive oil. Taste is essential to the overall flavor of a dish. I prefer extra-virgin olive oil because it is lighter in olive flavor.

PASTAS:

Semolina = Basic authentic style pasta

Fettuccine = Pasta made with eggs

Gluten-free pasta= Pasta made without flour

Whole wheat pasta= Pasta made with whole wheat for a healthier version of traditional pasta

CHEESES:

Fontina = Mild semi soft cheese

Gorganzola = Aged mild soft cheese

Romano Cheese (Pecorino)= Sharp hard cheese

Parmigiano = Mild hard cheese

Mozzarella = Soft mild cheese

Ricotta = Soft mild cheese

Provolone = Sharp hard cheese

Slicing Provolone -= Mild soft cheese used primarily for sandwiches

CHEESE AND GARLIC

Zuccarelli's always buys whole blocks of cheese, such as Pecorino, Romano, and Gorgonzola. The secret to great tasting cheese is to grate or crumble the cheese just before using it. Pre-grated cheeses are found in most grocery stores and are easier and convenient to use. However, pre-grated cheeses do not offer the superior taste. I recommend you grate your own cheeses when possible. The extra little bit of time is worth it! For the same reason, we never buy pre-peeled garlic, because by the time you want to use it, the flavor will be gone. Garlic will last a long time in the refrigerator as long as you don't peel it first!

MAKE YOUR OWN…

One of the best ways to enhance the flavor of your dishes is to make your own basics. My mother believes this is so important that we make basics in our kitchen every day. For the home cook, it can save money too. You pay to have someone else peel your garlic or grind up bread for breadcrumbs, and it just never tastes as good as it would if you did it yourself.

BREADCRUMBS

We make our own breadcrumbs using leftover Italian loaves or rolls from the day before. We put them on top of the oven so they get good and dry, and then we grate them, like grating cheese, until it becomes like a powder. We add our own seasonings. When we use it for breading on meat or fish, we mix the breadcrumbs with granulated garlic, grated Romano cheese, some dried parsley, and a little bit of black pepper. No salt, because the cheese already has enough salt.

People often say, "You have the best Chicken Milanese in the world, but when I try to do it at home, it doesn't come out the same way." So often it's because they're using inferior ingredients, like store-bought breadcrumbs, which hardly have any flavor.

ROASTED PEPPERS

To roast your own peppers, start by choosing really big red peppers with thick skins. They can't be the thin, long ones, because those don't have enough meat inside. Peppers hold a lot of water, and once they're cooked, all that juice comes out. If the pepper is too thin, there will be nothing left once it's cooked, and it will be very hard to peel them. You're not going to get the texture that you want.

Bake the peppers whole in the oven on high, at about 450 to 500 degrees, for about a half hour or so, just until they are a little soft to the touch and the skins get dark. Once they've cooled, peel the peppers and then clean out the seeds inside. You can clean out the seeds by cutting open the peppers, pulling out the insides, and then running them under water to wash out any seeds still stuck in there. Put the peppers in a colander to strain out all the juice. Transfer them to a bowl and add olive oil, fresh sliced garlic, salt, and pepper. Toss it all together and you'll have roasted peppers that are so much better than what you'll find at the grocery store.

My mother roasts a case of peppers a day to use at the restaurant. We use them for *Roasted Pepper and Mozzarella Salad* (see below) or *Caprese*, or just as a side dish on their own. Lots of people like to order them with their meat or pasta dishes. We also put them on sandwiches at lunchtime, like our Italian subs.

Marinated Eggplant

MARINATED VEGETABLES

My mom makes marinated eggplant, zucchini, mushrooms, and olives, which can be served as a side dish. At the restaurant, we often serve them as an appetizer on a plate with cheese, roasted peppers, dry sausage, and bread—food that you can pick at. We often bring a plate like that to the table just to say welcome to our customers. It's a little taste of how my mom ate when she was a girl in Calabria.

MARINATED EGGPLANT

Makes about 1 quart

3 whole medium eggplants, peeled and sliced lengthwise into ⅛-inch strips and then cut into ¼-inch wide strips

Salt

3 quarts water

1 quart red wine vinegar

1 long hot Italian pepper, small diced

5 cloves fresh garlic, sliced

7–10 leaves of fresh mint

Extra-virgin olive oil, to cover

LET'S START COOKING!

Place a layer of eggplant in a colander and then lightly salt it. Continue alternating layers of eggplant and salt until you've used up all the eggplant. Place a weight on top of the eggplant and leave it overnight to drain into a large stainless steel bowl. Toss the drainings.

Combine the vinegar and water, and heat on the stove until boiling. Add the eggplant and turn off the heat. Let the eggplant cool and then drain and squeeze it dry. In a stainless steel bowl, mix the eggplant with the remaining ingredients and a little bit of oil. Place in a jar, pack tight, and cover with oil. Refrigerate or store in a dark, cool place. The longer they marinate, the better they will taste.

Pictured on previous page.

OLIVE SCHIACCIATE (MARINATED OLIVES)

Three 32-ounce jars of medium fresh, raw green olives, cracked and pitted (available online or at specialty stores)

½ teaspoon fennel seed

Salt to taste

1 long hot Italian pepper, cut into small pieces

3 cloves fresh garlic, sliced

Extra-virgin olive oil, to cover

LET'S START COOKING!

After cracking and pitting the olives, store them in water. Change the water daily for 5–7 days. Drain well and squeeze out all water. Mix olives with the remaining ingredients in a stainless steel bowl. Place in a jar, pack tight, and cover with oil. Refrigerate or store in a dark, cool place. The longer they marinate, the better they will taste.

MAKE-AHEAD SAUCE

At the restaurant, we take pride in making our own sauces from scratch. I encourage home cooks to do the same. Many of the basic sauces, like marinara, can be made ahead of time and frozen for up to three months. This makes for a quick and easy meal during the week. The marinara sauce that follows is from an old family recipe that we have been making for generations.

KITCHEN TIPS

Don't overdo the fresh oregano. Sometimes, when people have extra, they like to just throw it in a sauce. But while a little oregano gives sauce a nice flavor, too much can make it bitter.

Forget about adding sugar to your sauces, too. Some people like to do it, but if you have good tomatoes, you don't need sugar. For a touch of sweetness in some sauces, we add carrots, minced very fine so they practically dissolve when cooked.

MARINARA SAUCE

Makes about 1 quart

¼ cup extra-virgin olive oil

¼ cup finely chopped onion

⅛ cup finely chopped fresh garlic

2 anchovies (optional)

One 32-ounce can whole plum tomatoes

⅛ cup chopped fresh basil

½ teaspoon sea salt

½ teaspoon freshly ground black pepper

LET'S START COOKING!

In a 6-quart pot, heat the olive oil over medium heat. Add the onions, garlic, and anchovies (if using). Sauté until the anchovies dissolve, about 10 minutes. Reduce heat to low and add the tomatoes, fresh basil, salt, and pepper. Continue to simmer, uncovered, until the sauce thickens, about 1 hour. Serve over pasta!

SALAD DRESSINGS

We make our own salad dressings, including a fabulous balsamic vinaigrette dressing that customers come in and buy by the jar.

HOMEMADE BALSAMIC DRESSING

Makes 1 quart

1 tablespoon Dijon mustard

¼ cup honey

¾ cup balsamic vinegar

1 tablespoon Ranch Salad Dressing and Seasoning Mix

½ teaspoon black pepper

½ teaspoon dried basil

3 cups extra-virgin olive oil

2 tablespoons water

LET'S START COOKING!

In a stainless steel mixing bowl, whisk together mustard, honey, vinegar, and seasonings. Slowly drizzle in olive oil to emulsify. Whisk in water and chill. Serve with antipasto, green salad, or just about any kind of salad!

EMULSIFY
Blend well to create a new texture.

Michael's favorite dressing

HOMEMADE TOMATO BASIL DRESSING

Makes 1 quart

2 egg yolks

16 ounces vegetable oil

8 ounces extra-virgin olive oil

6 ounces red wine vinegar

4 ounces chili sauce

1 teaspoon roasted garlic pepper

1 tablespoon dried basil

1 teaspoon garlic, chopped

1 teaspoon fresh parsley, chopped

LET'S START COOKING!

Make the mayonnaise base in a stainless steel bowl by slowly incorporating oils and yolks with a whisk. Add remaining ingredients and mix well. Refrigerate. Serve with green salad.

PIZZA DOUGH

1 18-inch pizza pie

2 ounces sugar

1 ounce salt

¼ ounce yeast

1 pint water

1 ounce olive oil

This recipe makes enough dough for an 18-inch pizza pie. It's easy to make, and store-bought dough often has such a terrible, cardboard-like texture.

LET'S START COOKING!

Mix ingredients together for 10 minutes. Put in a bowl and let rise for 6 hours. When you're ready to make your pizza, you can put the dough on a floured surface and use a rolling pin to make it round. Our pizza guy, of course, stretches and throws the pizza dough by hand, but he's been doing that everyday for years, so he's an expert!

FRANCES'S ITALIAN PANTRY BASICS

Fresh tomatoes—it doesn't matter what kind, as long as they're firm and ripe!

Basil—fragrant and green

Olive oil—it has to have that olive-y taste and color

Garlic—buy the head and peel it yourself for much better flavor

Hot pepper flakes

Fresh parsley

Onions

Ricotta impastata—a dry ricotta used for cannoli cream, Italian cheesecake, and calzones

Salt and black pepper

My dog, Valentino, loved the aroma of pizza in the oven.

PRESENTATION IS KEY

One time, one of our waiters was making an antipasto salad for one of his tables because my mother was busy. He was about to take it to the table when my mother said, "Hold it. Where are you going? Come back." He came back, and she redid the whole dish because the waiter hadn't put the tomatoes in right. "This is the way I want it to look," she said. "That's why I don't want anybody in this area, because you guys don't pay attention to what I'm doing. You've been here all these years and you still can't get it right."

That's why nothing leaves the kitchen until my mother inspects it, and if it doesn't look right, she does it herself. We're not into decorating food, and nothing we make is really fancy, but it does have to be pleasing to the eye. The salads have to go out a certain way. The lettuce, which my mother picks out herself, has to be the right color or it goes in the garbage. She's very particular about the details, but we think it's worth it.

Antipasto

Lettuce, romaine or iceberg, or a mix

Ripe tomato

White onion

Green and black olives

Pepperoncini

Sliced ham

Sliced salami

Sliced pepperoni

Thin-sliced prosciutto

Sliced domestic provolone

Cubed imported sharp provolone, which is a little harder than the domestic

Anchovies, optional

When we do cold cut antipasto plates, we slice the cold cuts ourselves and roll them a certain way, so the dish almost looks like a flower when it's finished. My mother is very picky about these plates and will often rearrange them herself before she lets them leave the kitchen.

TO ARRANGE

Start by rolling up the cold cuts. The meat can't be sliced too thick, but it also can't be so thin that it won't roll up well. That was actually one of my first jobs in the kitchen—to roll up cold cuts for the antipasto platters. Nobody liked to do it because it's time-consuming and tedious to roll enough cold cuts to serve an entire restaurant. Since I was the youngest, I often got stuck doing it.

Roll some of the cold cuts up pretty tight, and others a bit looser (you can roll those around your finger) so you can add an olive in the center.

Layer a bed of lettuce on your plate. We use a mix of romaine and iceberg. Then add the rolled ham and thin-sliced prosciutto (the prosciutto should be sliced a bit thinner than the rest of the cold cuts) and arrange those in a circle around the plate to make it look like a flower.

Add the pepperoni and salami with black and green olives inside, followed by slices of domestic provolone, which you can also roll around your finger and put an olive inside.

Next, sprinkle chunks of sharp provolone around the plate. Add just a few wedges of tomato on top—we usually put only three wedges. Add a few pepperoncini and anchovies if you like, and then top it all off with rings of white onion, but not too much. Serve with Italian dressing or our balsamic vinaigrette.

PROSCIUTTO
Italian cured ham.

CUSTOMER STORY

I have a regular customer from Boston who has been coming to the restaurant for about 25 years. When he hasn't been in town for a while, he'll call me up to ask, "How are you? How's your mother? How's your father?" He just wants to check in. Who does that?

He's very important to my mom. He'll walk in the restaurant, head straight to our open kitchen, and say to her, "Fran, where's my salad? You make my salad. You're the only one who can make my salad." My mom loves it. One time he was in with a friend who was stunned to see him walk back to the kitchen. The friend said, "What are you doing? Why are you going in there?" I said, "Don't worry about it, it's okay. He can go in the kitchen. He knows what to do."

ROASTED PEPPER MOZZARELLA SALAD

Fresh mozzarella

Ripe tomatoes

Homemade roasted peppers

Olive oil

Fresh basil

This is one of the dishes I have featured on the restaurant's website because it looks pretty when assembled correctly. Again, the ingredients are simple, but presentation is key.

TO ARRANGE

Slice the fresh mozzarella and ripe tomatoes into thick rounds. Arrange on a plate, alternating between slices of cheese and tomato. Add some roasted peppers on either end of the plate. Drizzle with a little olive oil and top with fresh basil leaves. My mother has a little herb garden with a basil plant growing on the side of the restaurant, next to our outdoor bar. She picks the basil fresh for this dish, and it smells so good!

CHAPTER THREE

FAMILY DINNERS MADE WITH LOVE

Family dinners were always a big thing in my family. We always had dinner at home, up until the time we opened the restaurant. Dinner was usually just the immediate family during the week, and then on Sundays the entire extended family would get together, all the uncles, aunts, cousins, and grandparents. When I was really little, everyone would come to our house, since I was the youngest in the family and my mother had to put me to bed early. When I got a little older, the families took turns hosting Sunday dinners at their homes.

Those family dinners were amazing. I looked forward to them because I always played with my cousins and that was a lot of fun. My cousins and I loved to play board games or go play outside in the yard. Although I am an only child, I was never alone. In fact, it almost felt like I had a million brothers and sisters. My father comes from a large family of eight and my mom also comes from a family of eight. Sometimes both families got together and there would be up to sixty or seventy of us. Now that's a big Italian family!

We had a long dining room table that would easily seat 12 chairs, and it felt like you could add a billion table leaves and keep stretching the table forever. The adults ate at the dining room table and the kids ate in the kitchen. We made a ton of food and just put everything out on the table so people could help themselves. Everyone had a favorite dish. One of my favorites growing up was my grandma Marietta's ricotta meatballs, a dish from my mom's hometown. When I was a kid, I used to watch my mother make the meatballs by hand. Watching her would make me crave them. We would eat them hot or cold, served with pasta or just as a dish by themselves. They're so soft and delicious. They are still one of my favorite things!

In my family, Sunday dinner wasn't fancy, but it was an event. The whole family would sit, talk, and laugh together all night. There was no hurry. If somebody showed up late, they'd just walk in, grab a chair at the table, and sit down. Everyone was always laughing and full of life. As with any self-respecting Italian family, everyone would be talking at the same time, so nobody could understand anybody's conversation, but that didn't matter because we were all together and happy. That is what truly matters!

After dinner, the women would go back into the kitchen, and the men would stay at the table. They'd drink homemade wine and talk about different things, old stories about back home, while the women cleaned up. Of course, I had to help too. My mother was always saying, "Okay, Olimpia, get up. Come help me do the dishes." I was always the dryer, which I couldn't stand. Since we didn't have a dishwasher, the women would clean the dishes as they went along with the dinner preparations (as I said before, cleanliness was a big thing in my family!). This was a good routine, because then we wouldn't be in the kitchen for hours cleaning after dinner was done.

Family included anyone who showed up for dinner at our house. People would come over, and there was always food in the house, so we'd put out cheese, soup or salad, olives, and bread. That became a meal. We called it peasant food. If we were at my grandparents' house, my grandfather would bring up gallons of his homemade wine from his basement cooler to drink. We used little glasses for the wine, what they call rocks glasses today. My grandparents never drank out of a stem glass.

Downstairs in the basement, my grandfather had what he called his cantina. He had his wine hooked up to a spout so you could just turn the spout and fill up a jug. When I was young, he used to send me down there to fetch the wine, saying, "Just turn the spout and bring me a gallon, go ahead!" But my mother was always afraid I was going to spill it all over the place. My grandfather always had wine. Sometimes he'd make white, but usually it was red. He'd make Chianti, Red Zinfandel, or whatever grapes he could get his hands on. It was easy drinking. There were no sulfites in his homemade wine, so you could drink a whole gallon, but then you'd have to take a nap afterward.

DINING ETIQUETTE ZUCCARELLI-STYLE

1. *Nobody eats until everybody has sat down at the table.*

2. *Before eating, everyone says* **buon appetito**. *Before drinking the wine, you say* **salut!**

3. *Always show respect. As children, we called all the adults "Aunt" or "Uncle" as a sign of respect, even if they weren't really related to us. We never called an adult by their first name. And if one of them said no, that we couldn't have something, that was it. You didn't ask twice!*

4. *Clean as you go. Nobody likes to spend hours cleaning up after enjoying a great meal, so in our house, you clean as you cook.*

5. *If you're late for dinner, just pull up a chair and start eating. We're not fancy, and family and friends are always welcome at our table.*

At the end of the meal, my grandmother would always put what we called the *macchinetta,* or the espresso pot, right on the table, and everybody would help themselves. Anisette, which is an anise-flavored cordial, went on the table—what we, even though we were all Catholics, called our holy water.

All those memories of family dinners as a child are still so special to me. I wish we had more time for moments like that. Of course, we're at the restaurant on Sunday now, so "family" means something different and includes many of our long-standing customers who we've known for years. Some of my favorite family dinner recipes are included in this chapter, which I hope you'll use to bring people together around your own table. It doesn't have to be about fancy dishes or a formal setting, just about good food and good company. That's the way it always was at our house, and I'll never forget it.

Stracciatella Soup

FAMILY DINNER RECIPES

Family dinners for us were about simple, shareable dishes. There were always lots of options, so everyone could just grab what they liked and help themselves. The most important thing was that everyone was together.

When the extended family got together for all those great Sunday dinners, everyone made something. (Well, all the women made something, since they were the ones who did all the cooking in my family.) We'd have simple dishes like peas and onions or potatoes, peppers and onions, lots of soups, and cold salads like tomato salad and string bean salad. And, of course, we had pasta. Pasta was always the first course for us. It was food that didn't cost a lot to make but that we all loved to eat. Italians call it peasant food.

SOUPS

STRACCIATELLA SOUP

Serves 1

10 ounces fresh chicken stock

1 cup fresh spinach leaves

¼ cup chopped cooked angel hair pasta

1 extra-large egg

1 teaspoon grated Romano cheese

½ teaspoon chopped parsley

Pinch of black pepper

Stracciatella comes from the Italian word *straccio*, which is like a ripped rag. Stracciatella soup is a kind of egg-drop soup with angel hair pasta and spinach. The egg is broken into the soup, so it almost looks like it's ripped, which is why we call it stracciatella.

LET'S START COOKING!

In a 2-quart pot, bring chicken stock to a boil over medium heat. Add spinach and pasta and let simmer. In a separate bowl, whisk together egg, Romano cheese, parsley, and pepper. Add mixture to the simmering broth. DO NOT STIR. Cover the pot and simmer for 2–3 minutes, then serve.

Pictured on previous page.

LENTIL SOUP

Serves 8

8 cups water

1 pound lentils

2 ounces extra-virgin olive oil

¼ cup diced bacon

¼ cup pancetta

1 medium sweet onion, diced

2 small carrots, peeled and diced

2 celery stalks, diced

1 tablespoon minced garlic

3 medium potatoes, peeled and diced

1 bay leaf

2 cups chicken stock

Pinch salt and pepper

This is an old family recipe for lentil soup. There are many variations of lentil soup from all over the world and from many different cultures but I believe my family's Italian recipe is the best!

LET'S START COOKING!

In an 8-quart saucepot, bring water to boil. Add lentils and lower heat to medium. Cook for 25–30 minutes. Drain water and let lentils stand. In another 8-quart pot, sauté bacon and pancetta in olive oil. Add onions, carrots, celery, garlic, and bay leaf, and cook for 1–2 minutes. Add chicken stock and potatoes and simmer for 10–15 minutes. Add drained lentils, and salt and pepper to taste. Continue to cook another 5–10 minutes and serve.

MINESTRA

Serves 4

¼ cup extra-virgin olive oil

1 ounce garlic, sliced

1 medium potato, cooked and cubed

1 head of escarole, chopped

1 head of savoy cabbage, chopped

1 stick pepperoni, cut into chunks

2 cups water

Pinch of salt

Pinch of pepper

Pinch of red pepper flakes

Note: Wash all greens first! Cabbage and escarole should be thoroughly washed, chopped, and rinsed before you start cooking.

Minestra in Italian simply means soup. This minestra soup is made of mixed vegetables with broth. There are many versions of this soup all over the world, but I think the combination of vegetables we use in this recipe is very tasty.

LET'S START COOKING!

In a 10-inch nonstick skillet, sauté garlic in olive oil over medium heat until golden brown. Add potatoes, escarole, and savoy cabbage while still dripping with water. While the greens are steaming, add pepperoni and 2 cups of water, and cook until tender, at least 20 minutes. Stir in the seasonings and serve!

PASTA FAGIOLE

Serves 6

2 ounces extra-virgin olive oil

4 ounces pancetta or bacon, chopped

3 ounces bacon, chopped

3 ounces garlic, sliced

¼ cup chopped sweet onions

¼ cup chopped celery

2 cups crushed whole tomatoes

1 cup chicken stock

2 cups cannellini beans, rinsed and drained

¼ teaspoon black pepper

¼ cup sliced fresh basil

2 cups cooked ditalini pasta

LET'S START COOKING!

In a 6-quart pot, sauté pancetta, bacon, and garlic. Then caramelize with onions and celery. Add crushed tomatoes and chicken stock and simmer for 40 minutes. Add beans, pepper, and basil and continue to simmer for another 15 minutes. Add pasta and serve.

PANCETTA
Italian bacon.

WINE THE ZUCCARELLI WAY

Wine was always an important part of our family dinners. Italians believe it's healthy and good for your blood, so we had it every single night. It was always on the table. Everybody drank wine in my family. When I was little, my grandfather and my dad would even mix it with Coke, ginger ale, or water so I could drink it, too.

*While we were eating, my grandfather would cut up peaches, or **pesca** in Italian, and dunk them in the wine. It was like an Italian sangria. The peaches would soak up some of the wine flavor and then, by the end of the meal, they'd be ready to eat. I used to love to stick my little fork in the wine glass to fish out the peaches. They were so good!*

VEGETABLES AND SALADS

BEET SALAD

Serves 6

6 medium fresh beets

¼ cup onions, sliced

¼ cup extra-virgin olive oil

Pinch of dry oregano

⅛ cup red wine vinegar

Pinch of salt

Pinch of pepper

LET'S START COOKING!

Boil beets in water for 30–40 minutes. Check tenderness with a fork and continue to boil until fork tender. Drain the beets and let them cool. When beets are cool to the touch, peel the skin and slice them. Place sliced beets in a stainless steel bowl and mix with remaining ingredients until well blended.

STRING BEAN SALAD

Serves 4

2 pounds string beans

1 ounce garlic, chopped

¼ cup extra-virgin olive oil

⅛ cup red wine vinegar

Pinch of salt

Pinch of pepper

LET'S START COOKING!

Prepare string beans by removing the center string and trimming the ends. Cut the string beans uniformly, wash in cold water, and drain.

In a 4-quart pot, bring 2 quarts of water to a full boil over high heat. Reduce heat to medium and add string beans. Cook for about 5 minutes, or until desired firmness. Remove from heat, drain, and chill the string beans before marinating in dressing. Finish by adding garlic, olive oil, red wine vinegar, and seasonings to taste. Toss, chill, and serve.

ESCAROLE AND BEANS

Serves 1

2 quarts water

1 teaspoon salt

4 cups fresh escarole, washed thoroughly

2 ounces extra-virgin olive oil

1 ounce garlic, sliced

3 ounces chicken stock

½ cup cannellini beans, rinsed and drained

Pinch of salt and black pepper to taste

½ pinch of red pepper flakes

LET'S START COOKING!

In a 6-quart sauce pot, bring salted water to a boil over high heat. Add escarole and reduce heat to medium. Simmer for 5–10 minutes, until escarole is tender. Drain escarole and set aside.

In a 10-inch nonstick skillet, sauté garlic in oil until light golden brown. Add chicken stock, cannellini beans, escarole, red pepper flakes, and salt and pepper. Serve.

CANNELLINI
Italian white beans.

PEAS AND ONIONS

Serves 2

⅛ cup extra-virgin olive oil

1 ounce garlic, sliced

¼ cup onions, julienned

½ cup peas

¼ cup chicken stock

Pinch of salt

Pinch of pepper

Pinch of red pepper flakes

LET'S START COOKING!

In a 10-inch nonstick skillet, sauté garlic and onions in oil over medium heat until golden brown or translucent. Add chicken stock and peas. Cook until the peas are soft or to desired consistency. Add seasonings and serve.

BROCCOLI DI RABE

Serves 1

2 ounces extra-virgin olive oil

1 ounce garlic, sliced

12 ounces broccoli rabe, washed and freshly chopped

4 ounces chicken stock

Pinch of salt and black pepper

½ pinch red pepper flakes

LET'S START COOKING!

In a 10-inch nonstick skillet, sauté garlic in olive oil over medium heat until light golden brown. Add broccoli rabe, chicken stock, red pepper flakes, and salt and pepper to taste. Cover and simmer for 5–7 minutes. Serve.

Note: For Penne Broccoli Rabe and Sausage, *after simmering the broccoli, add 8 ounces of sliced cooked sweet Italian sausage, and 5 ounces penne pasta, cooked al dente.*

Polpette Calabrese

PASTA AND MAIN DISHES

POLPETTE CALABRESE (MEATBALLS)

Makes about 20 meatballs

1 (6-inch) hoagie roll, cubed

2 pounds ground beef

3 eggs, lightly beaten

¼ cup minced onion

¼ minced garlic

¼ chopped fresh basil

¼ cup extra-virgin olive oil

Pinch of black pepper

Salt to taste

½ cup breadcrumbs

¼ cup grated Pecorino Romano cheese

¼ cup fresh chopped parsley

Meatballs, or *polpette calabrese* as we call them, were a popular dish in my family for adults and kids alike. They're popular at the restaurant, too, and we go through mountains of them. These homemade meatballs are good with pasta or just as a dish by themselves. Leftovers can be used for meatball subs.

LET'S START COOKING!

Soak bread cubes in water, then drain and set aside. In a large stainless steel mixing bowl, combine ground beef, beaten eggs, moist bread cubes, onions, garlic, basil, olive oil, salt, and pepper. Stir enough breadcrumbs into the beef mixture so that it's still moist. (Using too many breadcrumbs will dry out the mixture and create hard meatballs.) Add Romano cheese and parsley, and blend well.

Create each meatball using a large ice cream scoop. Place meatballs about 2 inches apart on a 9 x 11 inch deep-dish baking pan. Pour water into the baking dish until the meatballs are halfway covered. Add a teaspoon of olive oil and bake in a 425-degree oven for 45 minutes. Turn the meatballs once after 20 minutes, and then continue cooking until done. Remove from oven and drain into a colander. Serve with your choice of sauce.

Pictured on previous page.

EGGPLANT PARMIGIANA

Serves 1

3 slices of eggplant, peeled and sliced

1 egg, beaten

LET'S START COOKING!

Coat each eggplant slice in flour, then in egg wash, and finally in breadcrumbs.

OLIMPIA ZUCCARELLI

EGGPLANT PARMIGIANA (CONTINUED)

ingredients continued

Flour and breadcrumbs, as needed for coating eggplant

3 ounces extra-virgin olive oil

4 ounces tomato sauce

2 tablespoons grated Romano cheese

3 slices mozzarella cheese

In a 10-inch nonstick skillet, sauté breaded eggplant in oil over medium heat until light golden brown on both sides. Remove from the pan and place eggplant on paper towels to drain excess oil.

In a small sheet pan, layer the following ingredients: tomato sauce to cover bottom, eggplant, sauce, grated Romano cheese, 1 slice of mozzarella, eggplant, sauce, grated Romano cheese, and 2 slices of mozzarella on top. Bake in a 350-degree oven for 8–10 minutes. Serve over pasta of your choice.

PASTA AND PISELLI

Serves 1

⅛ cup extra-virgin olive oil

½ ounce sliced garlic

1 cup chicken stock

¼ cup peas

½ cup cooked ditalini pasta

Salt

Pinch of pepper

Pinch of red pepper flakes

Romano cheese and parsley, for garnish

LET'S START COOKING!

In a 10-inch nonstick skillet, sauté garlic in oil over medium heat until light golden brown. Add chicken stock, peas, and cooked pasta. Add seasonings and simmer for 5 minutes before serving. For a final touch, sprinkle with grated Romano cheese and parsley.

LINGUINI FRUTTA DI MARE

Serves 1

2 ounces extra-virgin olive oil

1 ounce sliced garlic

2 jumbo shrimp (size 6–8)

5 Manila clams

3 ounces sliced calamari

2 ounces dry white wine

2 ounces chicken stock

4 ounces fresh marinara

Pinch of salt

Pinch of black pepper

1 tablespoon thinly sliced basil

1 teaspoon butter

6 ounces linguini, cooked al dente

LET'S START COOKING!

In a 10-inch nonstick skillet, sauté garlic in oil over medium heat until light golden brown. Add shrimp, calamari, and clams. Deglaze skillet with white wine, chicken stock, and marinara sauce. Continue to simmer for 5–7 minutes. Finish with salt, pepper, basil, and butter.

Shock (reheat) pasta in salted boiling water. Drain the heated pasta and add to skillet with cooked seafood. Toss well and serve.

AL DENTE
Firm to the bite.

This is Jimmy Garlinge and me having fun in the kitchen

CHAPTER FOUR

QUICK-AND-EASY WEEKDAY MEALS

A lot of people think Italian cooking is complicated. But that is not the case when it comes to southern Italian cooking. There are different styles of Italian cooking which stem from different regions of Italy. The northern Italians have more of a French influence, and their style of cooking is totally different than the southern regions of Italy. Northern Italian cuisine has more complicated and richer dishes, using a lot of cream to make sauces. They also like to decorate their food. Southern Italian cooking likes to keep the recipe fresh and simple.

Southern Italian cooking is much easier to prepare, which is why it's so important to use fresh ingredients. And because it's simple, there are many dishes that can be whipped up quickly on a busy weekday without much effort. By and large, southern Italian cuisine is healthy, too. We use a lot of olive oil and fresh vegetables in most of our dishes. Since there are a lot of farms in southern Italy, the dishes often incorporate a lot of vegetables. My mother always jokes and says that she can survive eating only greens! You can do a lot with vegetables, garlic and oil, fresh tomatoes, and maybe a little sprinkling of Romano cheese.

The birth of new Italian cuisine began with the introduction of Italian immigrants to the United States. The New World Italian immigrants brought Old World traditions and recipes to America and paved the way for new and creative ways to make and introduce new Italian dishes, such as manicotti and lasagna. Dishes like these often have a long list of ingredients and are covered in sauce and layers of cheese. I love the traditional simplicity of southern Italian cooking, and I enjoy creating new recipes based on these traditions. I believe preparing an exquisite dish does not have to be complicated.

PLANNING AHEAD

One of the best ways to create quick and easy weeknight dinners is to organize and plan ahead. A lot of the basics that we talked about in the last few chapters can be made ahead of time and frozen until needed. This includes sauces, meatballs, and pizza dough. Roasted peppers, marinated eggplant, and salad dressings can be stored in jars and kept in the refrigerator. Pasta can be cooked ahead of time and kept in your freezer, too. Frozen pasta only takes a few minutes in boiling water to reheat. Now, you're just a few steps away from pulling together a great meal!

HERE ARE SOME IDEAS FOR QUICK AND DELICIOUS WEEKDAY MEALS:

PIZZA

Pizza dough freezes well (you'll find the recipe in Chapter 2), so it can be ready to use for a quick meal. Pizzerias will often sell you balls of dough if you don't want to make your own. We sell them to customers, too. Just ask! Once you have the dough, all you have to do is stretch it out (it doesn't have to be round) and throw your favorite toppings on top, and—presto!—your pizza is ready to put it in the oven! Our pizza is Neapolitan-style, which is thin crust, and it bakes in just a few minutes. Making pizza is a great way to use up leftovers, too. All sorts of things make good pizza toppings, including artichokes, sun-dried tomatoes, prosciutto, Gorgonzola cheese, arugula, spinach—and so on. You can use a little marinara sauce, too, if you like, or just fresh tomatoes.

MEATBALLS

Meatballs can be made ahead and frozen. (See Chapter 3 for the recipe.) Then you can make pasta with meatballs, meatball sandwiches, or even just have meatballs as a dish by themselves, which is one of my personal favorites, with just a simple salad on the side.

MEATBALLS, MEATBALLS, MEATBALLS

Every year we participate in the local Italian festival, where we get a booth and all we sell is meatballs and meatball subs. We make and sell 3,000 meatballs every year. I bring the meatballs to the booth in takeout trays, and we always get people who come to the booth and say, "Can we buy a whole tray of meatballs to take home?" So of course, I sell them a trayfull. We've been doing it for so many years now that there are people there who know me as the Meatball Girl.

JARRED TOMATO SAUCE

Some pasta sauces are quick and easy to make. Pomodoro sauce, for example, is simple and comes together quickly in the pan. All you have to do is add a simple mix of garlic and oil atop pasta and you've created a classic Italian dish. Sauté fresh vegetables in garlic and oil, throw some cooked pasta in there, and you've got vegetables with pasta in just minutes!

POMODORO
Fresh tomato, basil, garlic and oil.

CHICKEN CUTLETS

Chicken Cutlets are super quick. You just pan-fry them, and in a few minutes you can call it a day! Take a chicken breast, pound it to make it tender, then bread it (preferably with my mother's homemade breadcrumbs from Chapter 2) and pan-fry it like chicken parmesan, but without the sauce or cheese. This recipe is very healthy and very fast.

PASTA

Practically everyone likes pasta, adults and kids alike, and it's easy to keep it in the cabinet so you have it on hand whenever you need to pull together a meal quickly.

The marinara sauce recipe included in Chapter 2 can be made ahead and kept in the freezer. Or, if you want something really easy, you can pick up a jar of our home-style sauce (see sidebar).

Chicken Milanese

QUICK AND EASY RECIPES

OLIMPIA ZUCCARELLI | 85

ARUGULA SALAD

Serves 1

2 cups baby arugula

2 fresh tomatoes, large dice

1 medium sweet onion, diced

4–5 pieces roasted red peppers, cut into thin strips (preferably homemade—see Chapter 2 for my mom's recipe)

½ ounce extra-virgin olive oil

1/8 cup balsamic vinegar

Pinch of dried oregano

LET'S START COOKING!

In a large stainless steel mixing bowl, toss ingredients together until well blended. Then serve!

LINGUINI AND BROCCOLI

Serves 1

5 ounces linguini, cooked al dente

¼ cup extra-virgin olive oil

1 medium garlic clove, peeled and sliced

1/3 cup chicken stock

Pinch of salt

Pinch of pepper

Pinch of red pepper flakes

1 cup broccoli florets, cooked al dente

LET'S START COOKING!

In a 4-quart pot, bring 2 quarts of water to a boil. Once the water begins to boil, add pasta and let it return to a boil. Reduce heat and cook for 7–8 minutes until al dente. Once the pasta is done, drain the excess water and set aside.

In a 10-inch nonstick skillet, sauté garlic in oil over medium heat until light golden brown. Add chicken stock and seasonings. Bring to a simmer and add broccoli. Add cooked pasta to the skillet, toss well, and serve!

Note: For Linguini with Garlic and Oil, *follow the same instructions above, but omit the broccoli and add more pasta.*

BAKED ZITI

Serves 1

1 cup ricotta

1 large egg, beaten

½ cup grated Parmesan cheese

1/8 cup chopped parsley

½ cup grated mozzarella cheese

Pinch of granulated garlic

1 cup tomato sauce

8 ounces ziti, cooked al dente

Black pepper to taste

This is such a simple dish. All you need is ziti mixed with a little ricotta, parsley, and grated cheese. Our trick is to also mix egg in with the ricotta to give it some flavor. Put some mozzarella on top and bake it in the oven for an easy-to-assemble dinner with not a lot of ingredients.

LET'S START COOKING!

In a large mixing bowl, blend ricotta cheese, beaten egg, Parmesan, parsley, half the mozzarella cheese and a pinch of granulated garlic. Mix the ingredients until well blended. Add the cooked pasta and enough tomato sauce to make the mixture pink. (Reserve the remaining tomato sauce for the next step.)

Coat the bottom of a single-serving baking dish with tomato sauce. Fill the dish with pasta mixture. Cover with remaining tomato sauce and remaining mozzarella cheese. Bake in a 350-degree oven for 15 minutes or until the cheese is light golden brown. Then serve.

SAUSAGE AND PEPPERS

Serves 1

2–4 ounces sweet Italian sausage links

⅛ cup extra-virgin olive oil

⅛ cup red peppers

⅛ cup green peppers

¼ cup sweet onions

1 medium garlic clove, peeled and sliced

¼ cup marinara sauce

1 tablespoon fresh basil, sliced

LET'S START COOKING!

In a 10-inch nonstick skillet, evenly brown sausage on all sides over medium heat. Add garlic and continue to sauté until light golden brown. Add peppers and onions, and place sauté pan in a 350-degree oven to cook for 6–8 minutes. Remove from oven and add marinara sauce. Simmer for 2–3 minutes. Finish by adding basil, and then serve!

KIDS AND FOOD

Everyone knows that children are picky eaters. Because Zuccarelli's cooks everything to order, we can make food to satisfy any picky eater.

SOLE FRANCESE

Serves 1

1/3 cup vegetable oil

One 8–10 ounce fresh sole fillet

Flour, as needed to coat fillet

1 egg, beaten and mixed with grated Romano cheese and chopped parsley

Extra-virgin olive oil

1 teaspoon minced shallots

1 tablespoon butter

1 teaspoon flour

¼ cup dry white wine

Juice from ½ lemon

⅓ cup chicken stock

6 small shrimp

Pinch of salt

Pinch of pepper

Sole Francese is a quick and healthy option and one of our top sellers at the restaurant.

LET'S START COOKING!

Coat the fillet by dipping it in flour and then in egg wash mixed with cheese and parsley. Carefully place fillet in a skillet of hot oil and then turn over quickly. Continue to cook until light golden brown. Remove from skillet and place on a sheet pan. Finish cooking in a 350-degree oven for 4–6 minutes.

Using the same skillet, discard oil and then sauté shallots in butter. Add flour and cook over medium heat until flour turns golden brown. Deglaze the skillet with white wine, lemon juice, and chicken stock. Add shrimp and continue to cook for about 3–4 minutes. Finish by placing cooked sole in sauce with shrimp and continue to simmer for 3–4 minutes. Then serve!

DEGLAZE
Add liquid to loosen and create a sauce with glaze created while cooking.

CUSTOMER STORY

A quick meal doesn't have to be fast food. I have a customer from Philadelphia who comes every year. He calls me on my cell and says, "I'm coming in with my wife. I just want a nice quiet table." I say, "No problem." This guy just flies in, eats, and is out the door. But usually he calls later to say, "Another fine meal. Thank you so much. I'll see you next time I'm in town." He really appreciates being able to get good service and good food on a tight schedule. We make the experience at the restaurant pleasant and we always meet his special needs. This is why he keeps coming back.

CHICKEN MILANESE

Serves 1

1 cup fresh breadcrumbs

¼ teaspoon granulated garlic

Pinch of salt

Pinch of pepper

2 **chicken breasts,** trimmed and pounded thin

Flour, as needed to coat the chicken

1 **egg,** beaten

2 tablespoons grated Romano cheese

2 tablespoons fresh parsley, finely chopped

Extra-virgin olive oil

LET'S START COOKING!

In a bowl, mix together breadcrumbs, granulated garlic, and salt and pepper to taste. Set aside.

Place each chicken breast between two layers of cellophane, and, using a meat mallet, pound both sides until thin. Remove the cellophane and place chicken on a plate. Bread the chicken breasts by dipping them in flour to coat, then in egg wash mixed with cheese and parsley, and finally in breadcrumb mixture. Set aside on plate.

In a 10-inch nonstick skillet, sauté breaded chicken in oil over medium heat until light golden brown on both sides, about 3–4 minutes. Remove from the skillet and place on a sheet pan. Finish cooking in a 350-degree oven. Then serve!

Pictured on page 84.

POTATO, PEPPER, AND ONION PLATTER

Serves 4

5 medium Idaho potatoes, peeled, cooked, and cut

¼ cup sliced red bell peppers

¼ cup sliced sweet onions

Pinch of oregano

Pinch of salt

Pinch of pepper

LET'S START COOKING!

In a 10-inch nonstick skillet, sauté bell peppers, onions, and potatoes in olive oil over medium heat until potatoes are thoroughly cooked. Add oregano, salt and pepper, and serve.

Note: Caramelize the vegetables in the pan for the best flavor.

CHAPTER FIVE

CLASSIC ZUCCARELLI RECIPES PAST AND PRESENT

OVER THE YEARS, our business has evolved from an old-school Italian deli, where my dad made all of the pizzas and my mom cooked a few dishes, to a full-service restaurant with a full menu of Italian dishes. Our current restaurant has expanded even further, seating up to 150 people with an indoor and outdoor full bar. There is also an outdoor seating area where we offer live music and entertainment, which we can do all year round thanks to the Florida weather. Under my mother's supervision, we prepare some 300 dinners each night. When I finally realized that my place was in the family business, I started to focus more on the business end of running the restaurant, while my mother focused on managing the kitchen. I enjoy redecorating the restaurant every year, so that the restaurant ambiance makes every visit feel like something special. Sometimes redecorating involves changing the furniture or painting the walls, while other times it's a matter of changing the tablecloths and uniforms. To further enhance our customers' dining experience, we offer weekly live entertainment. I also take pride in my wine list and I am always adding new and exciting wines to the list. So even though we are a restaurant that's steeped in tradition, we are always finding new ways to satisfy our customers.

Despite our expansions and all of the changes over the years, we've always tried to make sure the place feels like home for our customers. Many of our longtime customers still come in and go right in the kitchen to give my mother a hug. If I'm not out front when they arrive, they will ask for me. Customers can eat anywhere they want, but they keep coming back to us because of the history together, and all the good times and memories that we've shared with them. We feel our biggest accomplishment is being able to make so many people happy for so many years. This feeling of accomplishment is what gets us up and ready to go everyday at the restaurant, home away from home.

WINE THROUGH THE YEARS

When we first started out, we were really just a beer and house wine restaurant—which basically meant that we served carafes of either white or red wine. That's the way it was for us in the 1970s and 1980s, until we started getting requests from customers for a wider selection of wines.

Our wine program is something that I introduced into the restaurant. I started to travel regularly to Italy and Napa Valley to learn all that I could about the different types of wine. I attended many wine tastings, learned about wine pairings, and developed a sophisticated palette. It was a natural thing for me, because I had always been interested in wine. I remember my grandfather making homemade red wine. The impressive collection of oak casks, coupled with the fermentation aromas of grapes and carbon dioxide gas, are forever etched in my mind. The wines would ferment and age until perfection, when they were ready to drink, and were always shared with family members and friends. Oh yes, pretty much just red wines in those days! You see, that was the Italian tradition in my family, as it was with many Italian families at that time.

I can remember at around the age of ten, sneaking down to the cellar when nobody was around, and stealing a sip or two of the homemade wine. It really did not taste very good to me. Eventually, I outgrew that phase and now I have become a real fan of wine!

During our deli days in Pompano Beach in the 1970s, we were serving foods like subs, deli platters, pizza, and, of course, elegant Italian pastries. Our wine program played only a minor role in the business, and we only carried gallon jugs of Chablis, Rosé, and Chianti. The only small bottles we carried were sweet and dry Marsala, imported from Sicily.

When we opened up the restaurant at Okeechobee Boulevard and Military Trail in West Palm Beach in the 1980s, we carried Chablis, Rosé, Burgundy, and Chianti for our house wines. We shifted from gallon jugs to three-liter bottles, but we still served the wine in unattractive, squat-stemmed Libby glasses with thick rims

CUSTOMER STORY

We have one loyal customer from Chicago, who was in the garment business. He and his family were Florida snowbirds who enjoyed spending the winters in their winter home in Florida. When he was in town, he would visit the restaurant often and would love to sit and chat with my mom and me for hours. As he got older, it became difficult for him to stand and wait for a table, so he would try to hand me a $20 or even a $50 bill to find him a chair, because he still wanted to come in and eat. I would always find somewhere for him to sit and he'd always say, "You're so good to me." One day, I received a big package in the mail from him, and when I opened the box it was full of new clothes. It was such a surprise! I called him up and said, "What are you doing?" He said, "Are you kidding me? That's the least I could do for the way your family treats me. I feel like I'm in the kitchen in my house when I walk into your place. I don't feel like another number." That sentiment made my day!

(continued from previous page)
Another time, when I was embarking on a new project for expanding the business, he signed his name to a $50 bill, handed it to me, and said, "This is for you for good luck. Hang it up." I hung that $50 bill on a wall in the restaurant and he was right, it did bring me luck! I will never forget him. When he became ill and couldn't travel to Florida as much as he used to, we would still call him to find out how he was doing. He was like family to us. I have learned that family is not necessarily tied to a bloodline in this world. He has passed away, but he will always live in my memory and I miss him.

(which never broke in the dishwasher, by the way). The wine was offered by the half-carafe or full-carafe, depending on the size of the party.

As the years progressed, we started offering a few premium wines by the glass, for our more discerning customers. As I learned more and more about wine over the years, our wine list grew. To accommodate this expanded selection of wines, I bought a wine closet so I could store up to 1,100 bottles. Our wine list has evolved to the point where we currently offer almost 30 red, white, and pink wines, and Champagnes and Proseccos, sold by the glass. This expansion enables our guests to make more exacting decisions regarding food and wine pairings. Our wine selection by the bottle has swelled to more than 200 wines, and they all sell.

Since my restaurant is all about family, I prefer to deal with family-owned and run wineries. Some of the wineries are owned and operated by large Tuscan families who have large real estate holdings, but continue to operate the family enterprises. I will always have a special place in my heart for some friends from Palm Beach, who own two winery estates in Radda in Chianti, Italy. Whenever I find the time, I try to visit wineries in California and in Italy and visit old friends, and also meet new ones. These travels are the lifeblood of my ever-changing wine list selections.

WINE AND FOOD PAIRING

The recipes in this book are the same successful family recipes that have been passed down through the years from southern Italy. A phrase we have adopted is "if it grows together, it goes together," referring to a long history of pairing food and wine from the same region. Today at Zuccarelli's Restaurant and Bar, you can enjoy a bottle of Super Tuscan wine served in proper Riedel stemware, which is a reflection of our wine list's refinement and variety. *In Vino Veritas*!

TIPS FOR CHOOSING AND SERVING WINE

Oftentimes, my customers will ask me to recommend a selection from our wine list. They trust I will select the right wine to pair well with what they're ordering. I love to pair wines with food in ways that bring out the best in both, the food and the wine. If you are choosing for yourself at home, selecting the right wine can be tricky. The rule of thumb used to be that white wine went with fish, other seafood, and salads, and red wine went with meat dishes and red sauces. But now, everything has changed. People drink white wine with meat and red wine with seafood. So how do you decide? The main thing is to drink what you like. Here are a few tips to help you choose and serve wine at home:

- *Think in terms of light versus heavy wines. A delicate dish, like seafood, is going to go better with a wine that isn't so heavy that it overpowers the delicate flavor of seafood. Depending on your palette, I would recommend a white wine or a lighter red wine. On the other hand, red meat or a spicy red sauce can stand up to full-flavored wines, while a lighter wine would probably get overshadowed by the flavor of the food.*
- *A common rule of thumb is "If it grows together, it goes together," which basically means that dishes from a particular region will generally go well with the wines of that region. That's one of the reasons I stock so many southern Italian wines at the restaurant. Our roots are from Calabria, in the south, which is where my parents are from and where my mother first learned to cook, so our wine list is heavy on wines from that region.*
- *Good doesn't mean expensive, so don't go by cost. There are tons of reasonably priced wines out there. What matters most is how it tastes and what your personal preferences are. For example, I know that I like full-bodied reds the best. In fact, Brunello, which is a super Tuscan, is what I call "my wine" because, for me, it creates the perfect pairing for most of my dishes.*
- *A general rule is that the older the wine, the more it needs to breathe before you drink it. At the restaurant, we use the*

guideline that if a wine is seven years or older, it should be opened at least an hour before serving. The longer the wine breathes, the more it opens up and the better it tastes.

- *To get a bit more specific, since many of the recipes in this book come from Calabria in southern Italy, a lot of them will pair well with full, super Tuscan reds like Brunello di Montalcino, Chianti, or Amarone. If you want a lighter red, you might look into a Pinot Noir. For whites, Chardonnays and Pinot Grigios are the biggest sellers at our restaurant.*

Veal Chop Boscaiola

EARLY CLASSIC RECIPES

I still have an original menu from our old restaurant in Margate, when we first branched out beyond being just a deli and pizzeria. Following are some of our favorite recipes from those early years.

VEAL CHOP BOSCAIOLA

Serves 1

For Veal:

2 ounces extra-virgin olive oil

14 ounces veal chop

Pinch of salt

Pinch of pepper

For Sauce:

2 ounces extra-virgin olive oil

1 ounce fresh garlic, sliced

1 ounce sweet onion, julienned

3 ounces mushroom, sliced

¼ cup chopped fresh tomato

6–8 sun-dried tomatoes, julienned

3 ounces brandy

2 ounces chicken stock

2 ounces heavy cream

Salt and pepper to taste

1 tablespoon butter

1 tablespoon flour

Boscaiola, in Italian, roughly means wilderness or woods. The name of the dish comes from the fact that it has mushrooms in it, which come from the woods, and features meat on the bone, which we think of as kind of rustic. It's served in a pink sauce that has sun-dried tomatoes and chopped fresh tomato alongside the mushrooms.

LET'S START COOKING!

Season veal with salt and pepper. In a 10-inch nonstick skillet, add oil and sear veal chop over medium heat until light brown on both sides. Remove veal from the pan and place on a baking pan. Finish cooking in a 350-degree oven until desired doneness.

In the same skillet, add oil and sauté garlic, onion, and mushrooms over medium heat until a light golden brown. Add both kinds of tomatoes. Let the liquids reduce, then deglaze the skillet with brandy and chicken stock. Reduce liquids again for 2–3 minutes. Add cream, seasonings, butter, and flour mixture. (The flour will thicken the sauce.) Reduce liquids for 3–4 minutes. Add veal chops to sauce. Simmer for 2–3 minutes and serve.

Pictured on previous page.

CHICKEN FORESTIERA

Serves 1

For Chicken:

1 chicken breast, trimmed and pounded

2 thick slices eggplant, peeled

2 ounces vegetable oil

Flour, as needed to coat eggplant

2 eggs

1 teaspoon grated Romano cheese

Pinch of chopped fresh parsley

4 slices mozzarella cheese

This dish is named *forestiera*, or forest, because of its fall forest colors. It's chicken in a brown sauce with purple eggplant and green capers.

LET'S START COOKING!

In a 10-inch nonstick skillet, heat vegetable oil over medium heat. Coat both sides of the eggplant slices in flour, then cover with egg mixture (eggs, cheese, and parsley) before placing in the skillet. Eggplant should sizzle in the pan. Brown on both sides, then remove and place on a plate. Set aside. In another skillet, sear chicken breasts over medium heat until slightly browned on both sides. Remove from pan and set aside with the eggplant.

CHICKEN FORESTIERA (CONTINUED)

ingredients continued

For Sauce:

2 ounces extra-virgin olive oil

1 teaspoon shallots, chopped

¼ cup mushrooms, sliced

1 tablespoon capers

2 ounces brandy

2 ounces chicken stock

3 ounces brown sauce

1 tablespoon butter

Salt and pepper to taste

For the sauce, add fresh olive oil to the skillet and sauté shallots and mushrooms. Add capers. Deglaze the pan with brandy and chicken stock and reduce for 3–4 minutes. Add brown sauce and seasonings and finish with butter.

In a 9 x 9-inch baking dish, create layers by alternating cooked eggplant, mozzarella cheese, and chicken breast. Bake in a 350-degree oven for 8–10 minutes and then transfer to a serving plate if desired. Pour sauce over the top and serve.

RIGATONI PASTORA

Serves 1

2 ounces extra-virgin olive oil

10 ounces sweet Italian **sausage,** casings removed

3 ounces heavy cream

3 tablespoons ricotta cheese

2 tablespoons grated Romano cheese

¼ teaspoon black pepper

5 ounces rigatoni pasta, cooked al dente

My dad chose the name for this dish. *Pastora* means shepherdess, and he chose the name because of the dish's white color, which comes from adding ricotta, a touch of cream, and grated cheese to pasta and homemade sausage.

LET'S START COOKING!

In a 10-inch nonstick skillet, add oil and brown sausage evenly over medium heat. Drain the oil from the pan and add heavy cream, ricotta and Romano cheeses. Reduce heat to low and continue to simmer for 8–10 minutes. Add pepper and cooked rigatoni pasta. Toss well and serve.

CHICKEN ARRABIATA

Serves 1

2 ounces extra-virgin olive oil

One 2–5 ounce chicken **breast**, trimmed, pounded, and cut into 1-inch wide strips

Flour, as needed for coating chicken (approximately ½ cup)

This is our signature dish from a long time ago. *Arrabiata* means angry, and the name suits this dish because it's very spicy. We sauté chicken strips with fresh tomato sauce, garlic, basil, mushrooms, and enough hot pepper to give it a good kick. Then we serve it over cavatelli pasta, which is an Italian pasta that's a little heavier than regular pasta because the dough is made with ricotta.

CHICKEN ARRABIATA (CONTINUED)

ingredients continued

1 medium Italian hot pepper, whole (optional)

1 ounce fresh garlic, sliced

1 ounce onions, julienned

2 ounces mushrooms, sliced

2 ounces fresh tomatoes, chopped

1 tablespoon capers

1 tablespoon toasted pine nuts

2 ounces dry white wine

2 ounces chicken stock

Pinch of salt and black pepper

1 tablespoon butter

2 tablespoons green onions, chopped

4 ounces Cavatelli pasta, cooked al dente

LET'S START COOKING!

In a 10-inch nonstick skillet, add oil, and brown flour-coated chicken strips on both sides over medium heat. Remove cooked chicken and set aside. In the same skillet, sauté garlic, onions, and mushrooms until light golden brown. Add tomatoes, capers, and pine nuts. Deglaze the pan with wine and chicken stock. Simmer and reduce for 3–4 minutes. Add cooked chicken breast to sauce and simmer for 3–4 minutes. Add seasoning, green onion, butter, and cooked pasta. Mix together well and serve!

(Optional: Sautee the medium Italian hot pepper in garlic and oil and place on top of the chicken as garnish!)

ARRABIATA
Spicy.

CHICKEN SCARPARIELLO

Serves 1

½ fresh chicken, quartered

½ cup flour

5 ounces vegetable oil

2 ounces extra-virgin olive oil

1 ounce garlic, sliced

½ cup sliced mushrooms

10 ounces (or 2 links) sweet Italian sausage, cooked and sliced

1 tablespoon flour

1 bay leaf

1 sprig rosemary

1 tablespoon capers

2 ounces dry white wine

2 ounces chicken stock

2 ounces fresh lemon juice

Pinch of salt and black pepper

1 tablespoon butter

Chicken Scarpariello doesn't exist in Italy, but it's a popular Italian-American dish served in the United States. *Scarpariello* means shoemaker in Italian. A lot of restaurants do it differently, but I like the way we do it because we use homemade sausage and chicken on the bone, which has so much more flavor than chicken breast. We served it early on in our restaurant, and we still serve it today. Customers will sometimes come in and ask, "Do you still have that shoeman's dish?"

LET'S START COOKING!

Coat chicken pieces in flour. Then, in a 12-inch deep fry pan, heat vegetable oil over medium heat and place chicken pieces in oil. Fry on both sides until golden brown. Remove from oil and place fried chicken pieces on a large sheet pan to finish cooking in a 350-degree oven for 10–12 minutes.

In a 10-inch nonstick skillet, add olive oil and sauté garlic, mushrooms, and sausage over medium heat for 2–3 minutes. Add flour, bay leaf, rosemary, and capers. Deglaze the pan with white wine, chicken stock, and lemon juice. Return cooked chicken to the pan and simmer for 8–10 minutes. Finish with butter, and salt and pepper to taste.

RIGATONI ZUCCHINI GRATINATE

Serves 1

2 ounces extra-virgin olive oil

1 ounce fresh garlic, sliced

1/8 cup sweet onions, julienned

½ cup zucchini, quartered and sliced

4 ounces fresh marinara sauce

2 tablespoons fresh basil, sliced

Pinch of salt

Pinch of black pepper

2 ounces grated Romano cheese

3 slices mozzarella cheese

6 ounces rigatoni pasta, cooked al dente

Gratinate, of course, means baked. So this is a baked pasta dish made with fresh zucchini.

LET'S START COOKING!

In a 10-inch nonstick skillet, add oil and sauté garlic and onions over medium heat until light golden brown. Add zucchini, marinara, basil, salt, and pepper. Reduce liquids and simmer for 3–4 minutes. Toss sauce with cooked pasta and add grated Romano cheese. Cover the top with mozzarella slices. Bake in a 350-degree oven for 4–5 minutes and serve.

GRATINATE
Lightly browned mozzarella.

Osso Buco

CURRENT CLASSIC RECIPES

Over the years, we've had a number of classic recipes on our menu that have come to be customer favorites. These recipes may be Old World, but they are also some of the most popular dishes currently served in our restaurant. Many of them started out as specials, but so many people ask for them that we've had to make some of them regular fixtures on our menu.

OSSO BUCO

Serves 1

¼ cup extra-virgin olive oil

2 tablespoons chopped onion

2 tablespoons finely chopped celery

1 tablespoon finely chopped carrots

1/8 cup minced garlic

1 (6-8 ounce) veal shank

1/2 cup flour

1 cup white wine

1 tablespoon unsalted butter

1 tablespoon beef base or 1 cube beef bouillon

1 large bay leaf

1 sprig rosemary

2 cups whole tomatoes, peeled

Salt and pepper to taste

One of my personal favorites is Osso Buco, an Old World recipe whose name means "hole in the bone." And that's exactly what it is—veal shank on the bone. We serve it as a special at the restaurant. Some people like it with gnocchi, but I love it with pappardelle pasta, which is a little lighter.

LET'S START COOKING!

In a 12-inch nonstick skillet, use half the olive oil and sauté onions, celery, carrots, and garlic. While cooking the vegetables, coat the veal shanks with flour. In a large 6-quart pot, add the other half of the olive oil and brown the veal shanks over medium heat until light golden brown on both sides. Add white wine, beef bouillon, bay leaf, rosemary, tomatoes, and salt and pepper to taste. Cover the pot and continue to cook over medium heat for 30 minutes or until the veal is tender. When ready to serve, add the unsalted butter and allow it to melt before serving.

Pictured on previous page.

OSSO BUCO
Veal Shank.

GROUPER PINE NUT WITH SAUTÉED SPINACH

Serves 1

For Fish:

One 6–7 ounce grouper filet

Flour, as needed to coat filet (approximately ½ cup)

1 egg, beaten

¼ cup pine nuts

Breadcrumbs, as needed to coat filet

2 ounces extra-virgin olive oil

For Spinach:

1 ounce extra-virgin olive oil

½ ounce garlic, sliced

2 cups spinach leaves

2 ounces chicken stock

For Sauce:

2 tablespoons butter

1 teaspoon chopped shallots

1 teaspoon flour

2 ounces dry white wine

2 ounces chicken stock

Pinch of salt and black pepper

LET'S START COOKING!

To bread grouper filet: Coat filet with flour, then egg wash, and then pine nuts mixed with breadcrumbs.

In a 10-inch nonstick skillet, sauté breaded filets in olive oil over medium heat until light golden brown. Place filets on a large sheet pan and finish cooking in a 350-degree oven for about 5–8 minutes. While filets are in the oven, use a separate 10-inch nonstick skillet to sauté spinach and garlic in olive oil. Add chicken stock and then drain and let stand.

Remove filets from oven and let cool. In the same skillet used to cook the grouper, sauté shallots in butter. Add flour and deglaze the pan with white wine and chicken stock. Add salt and pepper to taste. Reduce heat and simmer for 3–5 minutes. Place filets over spinach. Add sauce and serve.

Grouper Pine Nut

BUCATINI MATRICIANA

Serves 1

2 ounces extra-virgin olive oil

3 ounces garlic, sliced

4 ounces pancetta, chopped

1½ cups fresh tomatoes, diced

1 tablespoon basil

Pinch of black pepper

1 tablespoon grated Romano cheese

5 ounces bucatini pasta, cooked al dente

LET'S START COOKING!

In a 10-inch nonstick skillet, sauté garlic in olive oil over medium heat until light golden brown. Add pancetta and sauté until dark golden brown. Add tomatoes and simmer for 5–7 minutes. Stir in basil and black pepper. Add cooked pasta and cheese. Mix well and serve.

FARFALLE BIANCO ROSSO

Serves 1

2 ounces extra-virgin olive oil

8 ounces ground sweet sausage

2 ounces garlic, minced

1 cup fresh tomatoes, diced

3 ounces heavy cream

2 ounces fresh marinara sauce

2 ounces grated pecorino Romano cheese

1 tablespoon fresh basil, sliced

1 teaspoon butter

Pinch of black pepper

5 ounces farfalle (bowtie) pasta, cooked at dente

LET'S START COOKING!

In a 10-inch nonstick skillet, cook ground sausage in olive oil over medium heat until done and browned. Add garlic and sauté for 1–2 minutes. Add tomatoes, mix well, and continue to simmer for 4–6 minutes. Stir in the heavy cream and fresh marinara sauce. Finish with cheese, butter, basil, and pepper. Toss in pasta, mix well, and serve.

FUSSILI PUTTANESCA

Serves 1

2 ounces extra-virgin olive oil

1 long Italian hot pepper

1 ounce garlic, sliced

2 anchovy filets, chopped

2 ounces sweet onions, julienned

1 cup fresh tomatoes, diced

2 ounces dry white wine

2 ounces chicken stock

6–8 calamata olives

1 tablespoon capers

1 teaspoon toasted pine nuts

1 teaspoon walnuts

2 ounces fresh marinara sauce

Pinch of salt and black pepper

Pinch of crushed red pepper flakes

5 ounces fusilli pasta, cooked al dente

3 leaves chopped fresh basil, for garnish

LET'S START COOKING!

In a 10-inch nonstick skillet, sauté peppers, garlic, onions, and anchovy in olive oil over medium heat for 2–3 minutes. Add tomatoes. Deglaze pan with white wine and chicken stock. Simmer for 4–5 minutes. Add olives, capers, pine nuts, walnuts, marinara sauce, and then basil. Add salt, pepper, and red pepper flakes to taste. Continue to simmer for 3–4 minutes. Toss in pasta, garnish with basil and serve.

PENNE SICILIANE

Serves 1

2 ounces extra-virgin olive oil

2 anchovy filets, chopped

1 ounces garlic, sliced

3 ounces sweet onions, julienned

1 cup diced eggplant

½ cup diced fresh tomatoes

2 ounces dry white wine

2 ounces chicken stock

1 tablespoon raisins

1 tablespoon toasted pine nuts

2 ounces fresh marinara sauce

1 tablespoon sliced fresh basil

Pinch of salt and pepper

5 ounces penne pasta, cooked al dente

LET'S START COOKING!

In a 10-inch nonstick skillet, sauté anchovy, garlic, and onions in olive oil over medium heat until light golden brown. Add eggplant and sauté for 1–2 minutes. Add tomatoes. Deglaze pan with wine and chicken stock. Continue to simmer for 4–6 minutes. Add raisins, pine nuts, and marinara, and simmer for 3–4 minutes. Finish with basil, salt, and pepper. Toss with pasta and serve.

CHICKEN MEDITERRANEAN

Serves 1

For Layered Chicken:

2 ounces vegetable oil

Two 2–5 ounce chicken **breasts,** trimmed and pounded

2 jumbo shrimp, lightly pounded and tails removed

¼ cup flour (to coat shrimp and chicken breast)

3 slices mozzarella

4 roasted red pepper strips

4 ounces angel hair pasta, cooked al dente

For Sauce:

1 ounce extra-virgin olive oil

1 teaspoon minced garlic

1 teaspoon minced shallots

1 teaspoon flour

2 ounces dry white wine

2 ounces chicken stock

Pinch of salt and black pepper

1 tablespoon butter

1 tablespoon Oregenata breadcrumbs

LET'S START COOKING!

Coat chicken breast and shrimp in flour. In a 10-inch nonstick skillet, sauté both sides of the chicken breast over medium heat until light golden brown. Add jumbo shrimp, then remove pan from heat and set aside.

Assemble on a small sheet pan by layering the following: roasted red pepper strips, one slice of mozzarella, one chicken breast, one slice mozzarella, 2 jumbo shrimp, one slice mozzarella, and finally one chicken breast. Bake in a 350-degree oven for 8–10 minutes.

For sauce, use the same skillet to sauté garlic and shallots in olive oil over medium heat. Add flour and cook for 1–2 minutes. Deglaze pan with wine and chicken stock. Add a pinch of salt and pepper and finish with butter and breadcrumbs. Pour over layered chicken and serve.

Chicken Mediterranean

CHICKEN SILANA

Serves 1

2 ounces extra-virgin olive oil

One 2–5 ounce chicken breast, trimmed and pounded

1 ounce garlic, sliced

⅛ cup mushrooms, sliced

1 bay leaf

1 sprig rosemary

1 teaspoon flour

2 ounces dry white wine

2 ounces chicken stock

4–5 roasted red pepper strips

2 artichoke hearts

1 teaspoon capers

2 broccoli florets

Pinch of salt and black pepper

1 teaspoon butter

LET'S START COOKING!

In a 10-inch nonstick skillet, sear chicken breasts over medium heat until light brown on both sides. Add garlic, mushrooms, bay leaf, and rosemary, and continue to sauté for 2–3 minutes. Dust chicken breast in skillet with flour and deglaze pan with wine and chicken stock. Add capers, peppers, and artichoke hearts, and continue to simmer for 6–8 minutes. Finish with butter, and salt and pepper to taste, and then add broccoli at the end. Arrange on a plate and serve.

OLIMPIA ZUCCARELLI

CIOPPINO

Serves 1

¼ cup extra-virgin olive oil

1 medium garlic clove, sliced

⅛ cup zucchini, julienned

⅛ cup sweet onions, julienned

⅛ cup carrots, julienned

⅛ cup celery, diced small

2 tablespoons fresh tomato, diced

¼ cup dry white wine

1/3 cup chicken stock

Pinch of saffron

4 ounces mild white fish filet

4 scallops (size 10/20)

4 Manila clams

4 small or medium sized shrimp

Pinch of salt

Pinch of pepper

1 tablespoon butter

3 tablespoons peas

LET'S START COOKING!

In a 10-inch nonstick skillet, sauté garlic in oil until light golden brown. Add zucchini, onions, carrots, celery, and tomatoes. Continue to cook for 2–3 minutes until liquid reduces. Deglaze pan with white wine and chicken stock and then add saffron. While simmering, add fish and continue to cook for 2 minutes. Then add scallops, clams, shrimp, butter, and salt and black pepper to taste. Finish by adding peas and cover. Continue to simmer for 6–8 minutes until the clams open. Then serve!

CHAPTER SIX

HOLIDAYS AND SPECIAL OCCASIONS

Growing up, we always followed Italian traditions for the holidays, and we still do, both at home and at the restaurant. As Italian Americans, my family celebrates the traditional holiday of Thanksgiving, and we always have a turkey on the table. But everything else around it is Italian—the pasta, meat, and vegetable dishes are all dishes that my mother has been making for years.

At the restaurant, Christmas Eve is a big night for us, but for most of the other big holidays—Christmas Day, Thanksgiving, Easter, New Year's—we close the restaurant and take the day off so everyone can celebrate at home with the family. But, as I mentioned before, we define "family" very loosely. At our house during the holidays, the extended family includes good friends, friends of friends, and even customers who would otherwise be alone. All are welcomed to celebrate with us! We have known some of our customers so long that they have become family to us. At my house, it is not unusual to have thirty or more guests on any given holiday. My mother is always saying jokingly, "We work so much. When is someone going to invite us to their house for the holidays?"

LE FESTE DELLE DONNE

On March 8 each year, Italy celebrates Le Feste delle Donne, or Women's Appreciation Day. The event began after World War I, when men started giving the yellow mimosa flower to their female partners, friends, co-workers, and family members. A union of Italian women eventually declared that this special day should be set aside to celebrate womanhood, more specifically the importance of women in society and all the struggles and sacrifices they've had to endure to win their rights and freedom. As news of the celebration got out, it spread across Europe.

In March, when the event is held, the mimosa tree blooms, so the mimosa flower has come to symbolize Le Feste delle Donne, serving as a sign of spring, love, and hope. Today, the day is about celebrating equal rights and the true essence of womanhood. Since the restaurant is managed and operated mostly by women, we consider it a special day and celebrate it with a feast of our own, hoping that women of all ages will come and join us in celebrating themselves, and that the men in their lives will give them a mimosa flower, just to say thank you for all that they do.

The theme of Le Feste delle Donne is represented by yellow and white flowers. In Italy, women celebrate by going out to restaurants with their girlfriends. In West Palm Beach, you can take your girlfriends to Zuccarelli's and enjoy sharing classic Italian dishes with a glass of wine! The one food item that's a must for this event is the mimosa cake, which is a kind of sponge cake with cream frosting. It's traditionally decorated with bits of chopped up cake on top, which are reminiscent of mimosa flowers. During this holiday, mimosa cake can be found in most Italian bakeries, so buy one and share it with the women in your life!

THE FEAST OF ST. JOSEPH

Most Italian Catholics are very faithful to the saints. In Sicily, the saint that many people pray to most often for help and guidance is Saint Joseph. During the Middle Ages, there was a serious drought in Sicily, so a local woman started praying to St. Joseph for a miracle. In two days, the miracle happened, so now, every year in March, the Sicilians hold a feast and wear the color red to honor St. Joseph.

The Annunciation of the feast of St. Joseph takes place on March 25th. Seven days prior to that date, the Bible states that an angel came to Joseph to tell him that Mary would be giving birth to the Messiah. Today, Joseph is remembered as the man God chose to take care of Mary and Jesus, as the most blessed spouse, and as a true husband and father. The angel came four times in Joseph's lifetime to save them.

CUSTOMER STORY

A very special customer and friend has been coming to the restaurant for 25 years, since before my son was born. He was Jewish, so I'd ask him, "What do you do for your holiday?" He'd say, "What do you mean? I'm Italian." I'd say, "I know, you're more Italian than me." And he'd say, "Whatever I'm celebrating, I just want to come to your place and eat good food."

He lived down the street, so he'd come into the restaurant every week. He always brought in new business, coming in with parties of five, even ten people. He was such a loyal customer that for his 60th birthday, I had a plaque engraved with his name and put it on the back of one of our chairs. Unfortunately, he didn't make it to his 70th birthday. We were planning to monogram a table in the corner for him. He was such a good friend and loyal customer that he deserved it. He will always live in my heart and will always have a chair at my table!

ZUCCARELLI'S CALENDAR OF EVENTS

Most holidays the restaurant is closed, but there are a few exceptions when we celebrate the holiday by opening the restaurant and planning special events in celebration of the holiday so that many of our loyal customers can come celebrate with us.

- March 8: Le Feste delle Donne
- March 19: The Feast of St. Joseph
- December 24: Christmas Eve

SFINGE AND ZEPPOLI

Italian pasteries.

We celebrate St. Joseph's Day at the restaurant with a traditional feast as in Sicily. Nobody else in the area celebrates St. Joseph's Day, but I try to keep to tradition within the restaurant, and we have a great turnout every year. I serve all the traditional Italian foods, many of which are Sicilian recipes. The highlight of the festivities is when a priest comes and performs a blessing, which is very important because you can ask St. Joseph for blessings and goodness throughout the year. I build a pyramid on the table with all the food, and people just help themselves. We do salads such as eggplant salad, fish salad, and pan-fried artichokes. We serve meat dishes, seafood, and my mom's special tripe dish. Many of our customers specifically request my mom's special tripe dish when they come to the restaurant. Customers love it!

There are special desserts that are made just for St. Joseph's Day. They are called St. Joseph pastries. There are two different kinds of pastries that we serve, *sfinge* and *zeppoli*. We have a baker, an Italian man who bakes for us during the holidays because I don't have room at the restaurant to make all the pastries. We have him make between 300–500 pieces of pastry for St. Joseph's every year, and they're gone in seconds. Some customers come to the restaurant for the sole purpose of purchasing our St. Joseph pastries. The pastries for St. Joseph's are traditionally colored red, which is the color worn by everybody who is celebrating St. Joseph's Day!

We have a live band that plays Italian music, and we decorate the restaurant with Italian flags and candles. I also place jugs of red wine on the table for everyone to share in the celebration. Customers will get up and start dancing and singing their favorite songs. Everyone has a wonderful time.

Some of the traditional recipes that we serve each year include fried fish, veal *rollatini*, *arancini*, and pasta *con le sarde*, which is pasta mixed with a bunch of different vegetables, such as eggplant, fennel, and zucchini. The following are some of my favorite recipes that we serve for the holiday.

ARANCINI

Makes about 12 rice balls

For Filling:

⅛ cup carrots, minced

⅛ cup celery, minced

⅛ cup onion, minced

½ pound ground beef

¼ cup tomato sauce

4 cups cooled risotto (see recipe that follows)

1½ cups breadcrumbs

1 cup Romano cheese

2 large eggs, beaten

½ pound mozzarella cheese, shredded

Vegetable oil, for deep frying

For Breading:

1 cup breadcrumbs

½ cup grated Romano cheese

1/8 cup dried parsley

1 teaspoon granulated garlic

Salt and pepper to taste

½ cup flour

2 large eggs, beaten

Arancini are Italian rice balls that we make for the St. Joseph's Day feast and sometimes for the Christmas season as well. They are a traditional Sicilian dish, and Sicily is right next door to Calabria, where my mom and dad were born and raised. Not a lot of people make them, but they're very good and we have lots of customers who come in asking for them.

To make arancini, you start with a basic risotto, so a recipe for that follows this one. You can also use the risotto recipe as the base for a quick meal during the week.

LET'S START COOKING!

In a 12-inch nonstick skillet, sauté carrots, celery, and onions over medium heat until onions are translucent. Add ground beef and continue cooking until ground beef is thoroughly cooked. Remove pan from heat and drain the mixture of all the drippings. Add tomato sauce. Mix well and set aside to cool.

In a medium stainless steel mixing bowl, make breading by mixing 1 cup breadcrumbs, Romano cheese, parsley, garlic, and salt and pepper to taste. Ready the rice ball breading station by filling three containers with flour, egg wash, and breadcrumb mixture.

In a large stainless steel mixing bowl, mix cooled risotto with 1½ cups breadcrumbs, Romano cheese, and beaten eggs. Blend well. Using an ice cream scoop as a measure, scoop the risotto mixture onto wet hands and roll each rice ball. Make a deep well in each rice ball. Fill with meat mixture and cover with shredded mozzarella. Seal the opening with a dollop of rice mixture. Then, at your breading station, coat each rice ball with flour, egg wash, and breadcrumb mixture. Place back onto baking sheet. Repeat this process until all the rice balls are filled and breaded.

In a deep fryer, bring vegetable oil to 350 degrees (follow your fryer instructions) and place rice balls into the deep fryer a few at a time. Turn occasionally until golden brown, about 5 minutes. Place cooked rice balls on a paper towel to drain. Serve alone or with a favorite sauce.

SIMPLE RISOTTO

Makes 4 cups

½ **small onion,** chopped

1½ **cups of Arborio rice**

4 **cups water**

3 **tablespoons unsalted butter**

⅓ **cup Romano cheese**

Salt and pepper to taste

LET'S START COOKING!

In a nonstick skillet, sauté onions in 2 tablespoons of the butter over medium heat until translucent, about 3 minutes. Add Arborio rice and continue to sauté until all the rice is covered with butter. Add 1 cup water and continuously stir until most of the water evaporates. Add another cup of water and continue to cook. Repeat this process until the remaining 2 cups of water are used and the rice becomes tender but still firm and creamy, about 20 minutes. Remove risotto from heat and add the remaining 1 tablespoon of butter, Romano cheese, and salt and pepper to taste. *Note: If making rice balls, add a few threads of saffron while cooking the rice.*

Welcome to Zuccarelli's

CAPONATA SICILIANA

Serves 4–6

¼ cup extra-virgin olive oil

1 medium red onion, cut into small chunks

1 fennel bulb, trimmed, cored, and cut into small chunks

2 celery stalks, washed, peeled, and cut into small chunks

2 bell peppers (1 red and 1 green), seeded and cut into small chunks

1 teaspoon salt

Pepper to taste

2 dried bay leaves

½ cup vegetable oil

2 medium eggplants, peeled and cut into chunks

2 zucchinis, peeled and cut into chunks

¼ cup red wine vinegar

1 teaspoon sugar

4 sun-dried tomatoes, chopped

¼ cup capers

1 tablespoon dried oregano

2 tablespoons toasted pine nuts

LET'S START COOKING!

In a 12-inch nonstick skillet, add olive oil and sauté onion, fennel, celery, peppers, salt, pepper, and bay leaves over medium heat. Toss a few times, then reduce heat to low and cover. Simmer for 10–15 minutes.

In a separate 10-inch nonstick skillet, add vegetable oil and sauté eggplant and zucchini over medium heat until light golden brown on both sides, about 6–7 minutes. Remove eggplant and zucchini and drain on a paper towel-lined baking sheet.

In a small saucepan, bring vinegar and sugar to a boil and cook until syrupy, then reduce for 2–3 minutes.

When the onion, fennel, celery, and peppers are tender, uncover and add sun-dried tomatoes. Continue to simmer for 3 minutes. Sprinkle with capers and oregano. Add drained eggplant and zucchini and toss to combine. Then add the reduced vinegar syrup and pine nuts, and toss all ingredients for 1–2 minutes. Remove the bay leaves and serve warm or room temperature.

CHRISTMAS EVE

Christmas Eve is a huge event for my family. It's traditional for Italian Catholics to eat seafood on Christmas Eve, and the Feast of the Seven Fishes is an Italian tradition. But at the restaurant, we serve more than just seven fish dishes. Zuccarelli's continues this tradition by preparing and serving various seafood dishes using the freshest seafood available like smelt, octopus, *baccala* (which is codfish), and eels if we can get them.

We also include the traditional dishes, *pizza chiena* and *pizza di grano*, as they're called in Italy, which are meat pies and wheat pies. We serve them for Christmas Eve as well as Easter. They have a dense texture and almost look like cheesecake, but obviously they taste very different. You generally eat them cold, though they can be warmed up as well. We get them from a local baker to serve for the holidays.

Christmas Eve is also a big day for desserts, of course, and we put out a whole array of things, from pine nut or pignoli cookies and honey balls to strufoli, which is fried dough. Many of these things we've been making for the holidays since I was a little kid. (You'll find the recipes for some of these sweet treats in the next chapter.)

Following are some of our favorite and most popular dishes that we serve at the restaurant for our Christmas Eve celebration.

Zuppa Di Pesce

ZUPPA DI PESCE FOR ONE

Serves 1

3 ounces extra-virgin olive oil

2 ounces garlic, sliced

½ Maine lobster

4 ounces fish filet (your choice)

1 jumbo shrimp

4 each scallops (size 10–20)

3 ounces sliced calamari

3 ounces scungilli

3 mussels

3 Manila clams

3 ounces dry white wine

3 ounces chicken stock

5 ounces fresh marinara sauce

Pinch of salt and black pepper

2 tablespoons butter

1 tablespoon basil

5 ounces linguini, cooked al dente

LET'S START COOKING!

In a 10-inch nonstick skillet, sauté garlic in oil over medium heat to light golden brown. Add lobster, fish, shrimp, and scallops, and sauté for 2 minutes. Add calamari, scungilli, clams, and mussels. Deglaze pan with wine, chicken stock, and marinara, and continue to simmer for 8–10 minutes. Finish with salt, black pepper, butter, and basil. Serve over linguini.

BACCALA

Serves 1

For Baccala:

1 ounce extra-virgin olive oil

One 7–8 ounce baccala (cod) filet

¼ cup flour (to coat filets)

Baccala is a dried and salted codfish that we serve in a salad, fried, or in a red sauce. My mother soaks it in water for days and days and days before we cook it because it's so salty. In Italy, it's traditional to serve it for Christmas Eve, and people come in the restaurant every year hoping to have it for their holiday dinner.

BACCALA (CONTINUED)

ingredients continued

For Sauce:

2 ounces extra-virgin olive oil

1 ounce garlic, sliced

1 ounce sweet onion, julienned

1 cup fresh tomatoes, diced

6–8 calamata olives

1 tablespoon balsamic vinegar

2 ounces dry white wine

2 ounces chicken stock

2 ounces fresh marinara sauce

Fresh basil

4 ounces linguini, cooked al dente

LET'S START COOKING!

Coat baccala in flour on both sides. In a 10-inch nonstick skillet, add oil and lightly sear floured baccala on both sides over medium heat, then set aside.

In the same skillet, make sauce by adding oil and sautéing garlic and onions until a light golden brown. Add tomatoes, olives, and vinegar, and sauté for 2–3 minutes to reduce liquids. Deglaze skillet with white wine, chicken stock, and marinara sauce. Return baccala to skillet and continue to simmer for 7–9 minutes. Finish with fresh basil and serve over linguini pasta.

BACCALA
Codfish.

BACCALA SALAD

Serves 4

1 pound baccala

¼ cup extra-virgin olive oil

¼ cup fresh lemon juice

½ ounce garlic, minced

1 medium sweet onion, julienned

1 tablespoon capers

1 tablespoon green onion, chopped

1 tablespoon parsley, chopped

Pinch of salt

Pinch of pepper

LET'S START COOKING!

Poach the baccala in salted boiling water for 8–10 minutes. Drain and chill on ice. Crumble the baccala fillets into a large stainless steel bowl and mix with olive oil, lemon juice, garlic, onions, capers, green onion, parsley, salt, and pepper. Stir until thoroughly blended and then serve cold over lettuce!

FRIED SMELTS

Serves 1

6–8 fresh smelts

½ cup milk

1 cup flour

Pinch of salt and pepper

2 cups vegetable oil (for frying)

6–8 lemon wedges (1 for each smelt)

¼ cup tartar sauce

1 romaine leaf

SMELTS
A type of sardine.

LET'S START COOKING!

Begin by soaking smelts in milk for at least one hour. Coat each smelt with flour, and season with salt and pepper to taste. Fry coated smelts in a 10-inch nonstick skillet over medium heat until light golden brown. Remove smelts and place on a paper towel to drain. Serve atop a romaine leaf on a plate with lemon wedges and tartar sauce for garnish.

ANTIPASTO DI MARE

Serves 1

For Seafood:

4 small shrimp

4 scallops

4 mussels

4 littleneck clams

⅓ cup sliced calamari

3 ounces scungilli, sliced

LET'S START COOKING!

Poach all the seafood in salted boiling water for 4–5 minutes. Drain and chill with ice to stop the cooking process. Place in a large bowl and set aside for later.

ANTIPASTO DI MARE (CONTINUED)

ingredients continued

For Dressing:

¼ cup extra-virgin olive oil

½ ounce balsamic vinegar

Juice from ½ lemon

1 teaspoon capers

1 tablespoon calamata olives, diced

1 tablespoon roasted red peppers, julienned

1 tablespoon sweet onions, julienned

1 tablespoon cucumber, diced

1 tablespoon celery, diced

1 teaspoon garlic, minced

1 teaspoon green onion, diced

Pinch of salt

Pinch of pepper

In a medium stainless steel bowl, combine olive oil, balsamic vinegar, lemon juice, capers, calamata olives, red peppers, onions, cucumber, celery, garlic, green onion, parsley, pepperoncinis, salt, and black pepper. Mix ingredients thoroughly and add to chilled seafood. Let marinate for 1 hour. Serve over lettuce and tomato salad.

ZUPPA DI MUSSELS OR CLAMS

Serves 1

¼ cup extra-virgin olive oil

1 medium garlic clove, sliced

¼ cup fresh tomatoes, diced

¼ cup dry white wine

¼ cup chicken stock

12–14 mussels or clams

Pinch of black pepper

1 tablespoon fresh basil, sliced

LET'S START COOKING!

In a 10-inch nonstick skillet, sauté garlic in oil over medium heat until light golden brown. Add tomatoes and cook 2–3 minutes until liquids are reduced. Deglaze skillet with white wine and chicken stock. Add clams or mussels and continue to simmer, covered, for 7–9 minutes. Add black pepper and basil and then serve!

OLIMPIA ZUCCARELLI

Tripe

SPECIALTY DISHES

There are certain traditional specialty dishes that we make only for the holidays or for special occasions, like when a good customer is asking for them or is celebrating a special event like a birthday. Recipes for some of our favorite special-occasion dishes are as follows:

CUSTOMER STORY

We have some good customers who have been eating here regularly since we started. One of these customers likes to go fishing as a hobby. When he catches something good, he'll bring the whole fish to us and ask us to prepare it for him. We will inspect it first by smelling it and touching it to make sure it's okay—fresh and of good quality—and if it is, we'll fillet it and prepare it to order. Sometimes he'll bring in a group of people and a lot of fish, such as mahi mahi, and say, "We want it done four different ways." Satisfying my customers' requests always makes dining with us a special event!

TRIPE

Serves 8

5 pounds tripe (boiled until tender)

1 cup white onions, minced

½ cup green bell pepper, minced

½ cup celery, minced

⅓ cup garlic, minced

1 cup mushrooms, sliced

1 cup potatoes, diced small

¼ cup fresh parsley, chopped

¼ cup fresh basil, chopped

1 teaspoon salt

Pinch of red pepper flakes (optional)

4 cups canned crushed tomatoes

Tripe is a traditional dish in my mom's hometown of Aprigliano Corte in Calabria. Every region in Italy makes tripe, but they all make it in different ways. My mother makes her tripe like a stew. It's all cut up and served in a kind of red sauce with potatoes. My mother makes it by herself (she doesn't trust anyone else to do it), and sometimes we serve it at the restaurant as a special. We have a Rolodex of people who we know love it, so we call them when she makes the tripe stew, and they say, "Save me five orders. I'm going to have dinner there and then I'm going to freeze the rest!"

LET'S START COOKING!

In a 10-inch nonstick skillet, sauté onions, garlic, green bell peppers, and celery in extra-virgin olive oil over medium heat. Add diced tripe and continue to sauté until vegetables become soft. Add mushrooms and potatoes and continue to sauté for 10 minutes. Then add parsley, basil, salt, and red pepper flakes (if using). Add tomatoes and simmer until potatoes are done.

Serve with Romano cheese and parsley sprinkled on top.

Pictured on previous page.

THE RIGHT TRIPE

When my mom makes her special tripe dish, it has to be a certain kind of tripe. You can't just use any kind. There are a couple different grades, and she always buys the honeycomb tripe, which is the best. She soaks it in water for hours, usually overnight, and then boils it, strains it, and lets it cool off a little bit so she can clean it one last time before using it. She does all that because tripe is really fatty, and she likes to get every bit of that fat off before cooking it.

BRACIOLE

Serves 6

For Meat Rolls:

3 pounds flank steak

1 medium garlic clove, peeled and minced

1 cup parsley, finely chopped

2 cups grated Romano cheese

2 cups raisins

2 cups toasted pine nuts

Black pepper to taste

1 cup flour (to coat meat)

2 quarts fresh marinara sauce

I prepare the braciole, which are Italian stuffed beef rolls. The braciole recipe was originally my mother's recipe, but about 15 years ago she got tired of doing it because it is very time-consuming, so she taught me how to prepare the recipe. Just like with my mom's tripe, we have customers who wait for us to make this special dish. We call them when we are going to offer braciole as a special for the day and they come.

Braciole is another peasant dish from the Calabria region that hardly anyone makes anymore because it has multiple steps and takes a while to cook. That's why I only make it once in a while, for holidays or as a special. You have to trim and pound the meat, then stuff it, roll it, and secure it with long toothpicks or kitchen twine. I pan fry it just a little to brown it and then use the drippings in the pan to make a red sauce from scratch that has the flavor of the meat. Then it cooks for about an hour until it's tender. We serve it over pappardelle pasta or sometimes over gnocchi or cavatelli, depending on what I feel like. A lot of times, people want it over risotto, but I don't like it that way as much

BRACIOLE (CONTINUED)

ingredients continued

For Sauce:

¾ cup extra-virgin olive oil

1 garlic clove

1 cup sweet onions, chopped

½ cup dry red wine

1 bay leaf

Sliced fresh basil

2 quarts canned whole or crushed tomatoes

Pinch of salt

Pinch of pepper

because it makes it really heavy and I think it sort of obscures the taste of the meat. I want you to taste the meat, so I like to pair it with something lighter.

LET'S START COOKING!

Trim, slice, and pound the flank steak until thin. Lay out the steak scaloppini-style. Sprinkle with minced garlic, parsley, cheese, raisins, pine nuts, and black pepper. Fold over sides and roll it up, securing it closed with a toothpick or by tying it with butcher twine. Evenly coat bracioles in flour. In a large deep pan, sauté coated bracioles in oil until evenly brown. Remove from oil and set aside.

To make sauce, sauté garlic and onions in oil until light golden brown. Deglaze skillet with red wine. Add tomatoes and seasonings. Add bracioles to the skillet and cover. Braise (simmer) for 1 hour or until meat is tender. Stir in marinara sauce. Remove toothpicks and serve over pasta.

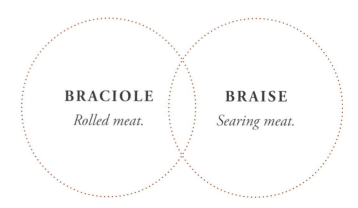

BRACIOLE
Rolled meat.

BRAISE
Searing meat.

Braciole

CUSTOMER STORY

One of the best parts of being in the restaurant business is being able to help customers celebrate special events. I'm always appreciative when customers choose to have their special moments in my restaurant. I couldn't tell you how many marriage proposals we've had over the years (because there are so many!). I do have a very fond recollection of one very special moment when the son of some special customers, who have been coming in for years, came to me and said, "Olimpia, you're like my sister. I'm going to propose to my girlfriend tonight. Would it be possible, when I come in, if you could just meet me at the counter? I want to give you the ring, and I want you to put it in her favorite dessert, which is your ricotta cheesecake!"

Of course, I said no problem. At the end of the meal, I could tell he was so nervous. I was walking around waiting for his signal, and then he looked at me and winked, and I knew he was ready. So I put the ring in a little parchment paper and hid it in the cheesecake. I brought this special dessert to the table along with their cappuccinos. She began eating the cheesecake when, all of a sudden she saw the paper and pulled it out of the cheesecake with a look of surprise! As she opened the paper and uncovered the beautiful engagement ring, he got down on his knee and proposed. It was amazing to see such a beautiful couple, so in love! Of course, she said yes and now they've been married about 10 years. When it was happening, I just stood there watching and thinking, "Wow, look at these good things that happen in our place!"

CHAPTER SEVEN

SWEETS AND AFTER-DINNER TREATS

SOME OF MY FAVORITE childhood memories were of the sweet treats available only in wintertime. When the first snow came down, my mom would go outside and get a bunch of fresh clean snow. With it, she'd make a kind of slush or slurpee by adding sweet syrup her mother made from leftover figs and honey. We called it scirubetta, and we used to eat it with a spoon. What a great memory! I would never change my childhood for anything. Because of memories like this and the sweet innocence of times gone by, I could easily live that past again.

Dessert was always a big part of our family dinner. It is a true extension of the meal. We would put all sorts of treats on the table and everybody would just help themselves, as we did with the main dishes. There was hardly ever any formal table service; there were simply a great variety of dishes from which everyone could partake and enjoy.

At our family's dinner table, there always were so many homemade delights to be had, including many different cookies and biscotti. There were always multiple options on the table, and everything was homemade. My mother, my grandmother, and my aunts always made assorted biscotti and little pastries called *pasticiotti*, which look like little pies filled with jelly. They weren't sugary sweet, because we're not big on really sweet desserts, but they were delicious.

A centerpiece on the dinner table was a nutcracker, because in addition to all the baked goods, fresh unshelled nuts like walnuts and pecans were also included with dessert. My grandfather used to have fig trees in Italy and he continued to grow fig trees in Westchester, as well. Figs were often on the dessert table along with whatever kind of fresh

SCIRUBETTA
Homemade Italian ice.

PASTICIOTTI
Italian pastry.

OLIMPIA ZUCCARELLI | 157

fruit was in season, like peaches (often soaked in homemade wine), pears, nectarines, tangerines, lots of apples, and a plethora of grapes.

La macchinetta, which is the old espresso pot, always went on the table along with the desserts. We'd make American coffee if we had guests, but usually we just made espresso. My mom's family had goats on their farm in Calabria, but not cows, so they didn't have access to cow's milk. On occasion, they drank goat's milk. At home, we always made espresso, and we still prefer our coffee that way. However, we do serve a wonderful cappuccino in the restaurant, and now and then I indulge in a fresh cup.

Of course, sweets are an important part of our menu at the restaurant as well. All year round, we make traditional desserts daily, like our ricotta cheesecake, tiramisu, and cannoli. For the holidays, we always have extra things to offer, like pignoli cookies and plenty of biscotti. Following are some of our favorite sweet treat recipes.

CORDIALS

*Italians have a lot of choices for settling their stomachs. In addition to sweet treats, another important part of the dessert table is some type of cordial— either a **digestivo** or **apperitivo**. Cordials are traditionally served in Italy to settle the stomach and aid in digestion either before (with apperitivos) or after (with digestivos) a meal. These are some of the favorites that I grew up with and which we offer in our restaurant. We typically serve them in a snifter, either neat or on the rocks, depending on what the customers prefer. Cordials are good for the stomach and digestion and serve as a wonderful beginning or ending to a great dinner!*

Bitters, *digestivo*
Amaro means bitter in Italian and this after-dinner digestif has a bitter herbal flavor.

Chinotto, *apperitivo*
Chinotto is a dark citrus-flavored carbonated drink that I like to serve over ice. It's fizzy, almost like a Coca-Cola.

Anisette, *digestivos*
After coffee or with coffee Both are sweet, anise-flavored liqueurs that pair well with an after-dinner coffee.

CROCHETTE

1 pound white figs

½ cup walnuts, shelled and halved

1/8 cup sugar

Crochette is a quick dessert of nuts stuffed inside figs. When I was young, my mother would bake them in the oven to get them nice and hot, and then put sugar on them. We'd cool them off and eat them just like that. It was so simple and so delicious.

LET'S START COOKING!

Cut whole figs nearly in half, but not completely. They should resemble a butterfly when you split them open. Place one open, butterflied fig directly on top of another so that the two figs create a crisscross pattern. Fill the center with a few walnut halves and seal the figs together by lightly pressing the sides together with the palm of your hand. Continue filling remaining figs until you've used them all.

Place walnut-filled figs on a baking sheet. Bake in a 350-degree oven for about 10 minutes or until golden brown. While the figs are still warm, sprinkle sugar over the top and serve.

RICOTTA CHEESECAKE

For Cheesecake:

12 eggs

3 pounds (48 ounces) **impastata** (dry ricotta)

1 cup confectionery sugar

½ cup Italian herb liqueur

½ cup Triple Sec

1 teaspoon vanilla

Finely grated zest from 1 lemon

Finely grated zest from 1 orange

For Crust:

1½ cups graham cracker crumbs

¼ **stick butter,** melted

For the Italian cheesecake, you have to use ricotta impastata, which is the dry ricotta. You can't use regular ricotta because it has too much liquid and the cheesecake will become soggy and fall apart. I also recommend using confectionery sugar instead of regular sugar. Zuccarelli's uses shaved orange and lemon zest in the cheesecake to give it a special flavor.

Note: You'll need a 10-inch round, nonstick springform pan for this recipe.

LET'S START COOKING!

In a large stainless steel bowl, whisk together eggs, ricotta cheese, sugar, Strega, Triple Sec, vanilla, lemon zest, and orange zest. Continue whisking until all ingredients are well blended. Let mixture rest for 10 minutes and then set aside.

Prepare your springform pan by covering the sides and bottom with melted butter. Create the crust by using your fingers to press graham cracker crumbs evenly across the bottom and sides until covered. Put in freezer to firm for 10 minutes.

Finish by gently pouring the ricotta mixture on top of the graham cracker crust. Bake in a 350-degree oven for 2 hours or until top is light golden brown. Chill overnight and then serve.

THE RIGHT RICOTTA

For cannoli cream and cheesecake, be sure to use impastata, which is a dry ricotta. Regular ricotta cheese that is sold next to cottage cheese at most grocery stores should not be used. Impastata can be ordered and bought at most Italian grocery stores. If you don't use impastata, then the cream will be too watery and too loose. You must have the thicker consistency to hold everything together.

TIRAMISU

Two 16-ounce packages of lady finger cookies, toasted and cooled

¾ cup espresso coffee, cold (to sprinkle on cookies)

Hazelnut Liqueur or Irish Cream (to sprinkle on cookies as needed)

¾ cup sugar

2 cups mascarpone

8 eggs, separated

1 cup semisweet chocolate, grated

For the tiramisu, it's best to use mascarpone cheese, not cream cheese. A lot of people improvise and use cream cheese, but cream cheese alters the flavor and texture of the traditional tiramisu. Zuccarelli's only uses the finest dark chocolate to offset the sweetness. Although cocoa or milk chocolate can be used instead of dark chocolate, it will change the subtle flavor of the tiramisu.

LET'S START COOKING!

Toast lady finger cookies and then drizzle with chilled espresso coffee, hazelnut liquor, or Irish Cream until cookies are wet but NOT soaked. Set aside.

In a large stainless steel bowl, mix sugar and mascarpone until well blended. Add egg yolks one at a time, and, using an electric mixer, beat until smooth and creamy.

In a separate bowl, beat egg whites with an electric mixer until very stiff peaks form. Gently fold egg whites into the mascarpone mixture. Continue to gently blend until a custard forms.

In a 9 x 11 baking dish, assemble ingredients: Begin with a layer of lady fingers placed flat crust-side up. Then completely cover the lady fingers with the mascarpone mixture. Sprinkle a layer of grated semisweet chocolate on top. Repeat these steps until you've filled the baking dish or used all the ingredients. Finish with grated semisweet chocolate on top. Chill overnight and serve!

CANNOLI

Serves 16

5 pounds impastata (dry ricotta)

1 cup sugar

½ cup Italian herb liqueur

7 drops cinnamon oil

1 cup semisweet chocolate mini-morsels

16 cannoli shells

Powdered sugar, for garnish

LET'S START COOKING!

In a large stainless steel mixing bowl, whisk together all ingredients until combined. Use a pastry bag with a medium tip to fill cannoli shells with filling. Sprinkle with powdered sugar and serve.

STRUFOLI

4 to 5 cups unsifted all-purpose flour

2 teaspoons baking powder

1 teaspoon salt

3 tablespoons white wine

¼ cup vegetable oil

6 eggs, beaten

Honey and sprinkles, for garnish

LET'S START COOKING!

In a sifter, blend flour, baking powder, and salt on a pastry board. Create a well in the center of the flour mixture and add white wine, vegetable oil, and beaten eggs. Using a fork, gently blend all the ingredients together until dough is formed. Knead the dough on the pastry board until soft and smooth. Roll into a large ball and then cut it in half. Place one half of the dough under a damp cloth to prevent it from drying.

On a clean, well-floured surface, use a rolling pin to roll out the other half of the dough to a ¼-inch thickness. Cut the flattened dough into ½-inch wide strips. With the palms of your hands, roll each strip into the shape of a pencil. Cut the pencil-shaped dough into ¼-inch pieces. In a deep fryer, bring oil to a medium heat. Deep-fry each piece until deep golden brown. Let cool. Repeat process with other half of dough. Add honey and sprinkles. Then serve!

OLIMPIA ZUCCARELLI | 165

FRANCES'S LIMONCELLO

Why do customers come to Zuccarelli's? Because they know I am here every day and that I treat all my customers like family. At Zuccarelli's, my customers are not just another number, and I strive to give them a great dining experience. Whenever I can, I like to surprise my customers with a little something extra. At the end of the night, I often give a shot of my mom's special homemade limoncello to our customers. I bring the shots to the table, and I say, "Thank you for coming here. Thank you for choosing Zuccarelli's!" There are many restaurants in West Palm Beach to choose from, but none of them can offer my mother's homemade Limoncello.

My mother has made her own limoncello for years. She learned how to make it from a good friend who came from Istria, on the outskirts of Naples. She says it's time-consuming, but it's not hard to make. If you're adventurous, follow these instructions (in her own words):

LET'S START COOKING!

Get a bottle of grain alcohol and 14 very yellow lemons. They have to be sun-kissed lemons. Very yellow, yellow, yellow not green…yellow! The lemon has to be completely yellow with no spots of green. The lemons cannot be pale either, only bright fresh yellow! They also have to have a sweet tart lemon scent, and the skin should feel smooth.

Take a really sharp potato peeler and peel off the skin of the lemons. You don't want any of the white pulp underneath that's attached to the peel; otherwise, it's going to be bitter. So you have to do it very gently to make sure you have just a very thin layer of the yellow rind.

Then, put the peels from all the lemons (keep the fruit for something else) into the alcohol. (You're going to have to either split up the alcohol into two bottles so you have room for the lemon peel, or find a big container to put it all in.) Close up the bottles or container and let the peels sit in the alcohol for a week. The alcohol will turn a yellow color.

Make a simple syrup by combining 2½ pounds of sugar with 1½ liters of water in a pot and boiling it until all the sugar dissolves and it thickens. Mix that with the alcohol with the lemon peels.

Store the limoncello in clear bottles so you can see the peels and the lovely yellow color. Serve it straight from the freezer—it has to be ice cold—after the meal in little shot glasses. The glasses should be chilled in the freezer before serving as well.

ADVICE FOR ASPIRING RESTAURANT OWNERS

The restaurant business is not an easy pursuit. The nature of the business is very competitive, and most restaurants fail. In many ways we're not too different from other restaurants, but one of the biggest differences is that my mother and I are hands-on owners. We have learned the skills and can do all the work required to run a restaurant. I believe that to be successful, you must know everything that's going on in your business. What are you going to do if the line guy doesn't show up? Because I am a hands-on owner, I get behind the line and cook the dishes myself. When people ask, "What's the key to your success?" I say, "Being on the premises all the time." You have to be there protecting your name and your investment. Zuccarelli's has been in business for more than 30 years. Our name is on the building and serves as a testimony to our success!

Part of building a successful restaurant is hiring a reliable and competent staff. We are blessed at Zuccarelli's to have such a wonderful team! As the owner and manager of Zuccarelli's, I wear many hats. At times, I have to wear my movie director hat and motivate my staff before the doors open by saying, "It's show time! Just remember, when you look bad, I look bad. I'm only as good as you are." I also have to wear my keeper of the peace hat. One of these days I'm going to be dressed in black and white, with a whistle around my neck, wearing my referee hat! I also have to wear a diplomat hat when I talk to people. Zuccarelli's has an open-door policy, and if someone who works for me has something to say, we go in the office and discuss the problem and find solutions. I want my employees to feel comfortable putting their thoughts and ideas on the table for discussion; however, my employees recognize that I am responsible for making any final decisions.

I hope my cookbook serves as an inspiration, and if you decide to become a restaurateur, I wish you luck and a successful journey!

ENJOY LIFE, ENJOY ZUCCARELLI'S

When you work this much, you also have to keep a sense of humor. We are always laughing at Zuccarelli's. At the end of the day, it's a dish of pasta. It's a piece of fish. It's a side of meatballs. Although it is common knowledge that you can't please everybody all the time, at Zuccarelli's we never stop trying! We work hard to earn people's appreciation and loyalty. When we see customers react with pleasure the way they do, it just makes it all worthwhile. It's the satisfaction of being paid a compliment, when people tell us they love it at Zuccarelli's, or when they recommend us to their friends and family to have dinner here because it has been such a great experience. The key to success, the whole idea, is to get customers to come back again. And again. And again. Loyal customers are the foundation of a successful business!

AFTERWORD

A Chair at My Table is my personal reflection spanning 30 years of operating and managing my restaurant, Zuccarelli's.

I am currently developing a consultation firm that will provide educational opportunities to help women follow their entrepreneurial dreams. I am also planning my trip across the country to host lectures, demonstrations, and book signing events. In the mean time, I will continue managing and operating Zuccarelli's in West Palm Beach with the help and support of my mother, Frances.

I would like to thank my fans and remind everyone that there will be another chair at my table soon.

I'm looking forward to sharing the next cookbook full of new and exciting recipes with you soon!

Living – Loving – Dreaming – Zuccarelli

XOXO,
Olimpia Zuccarelli

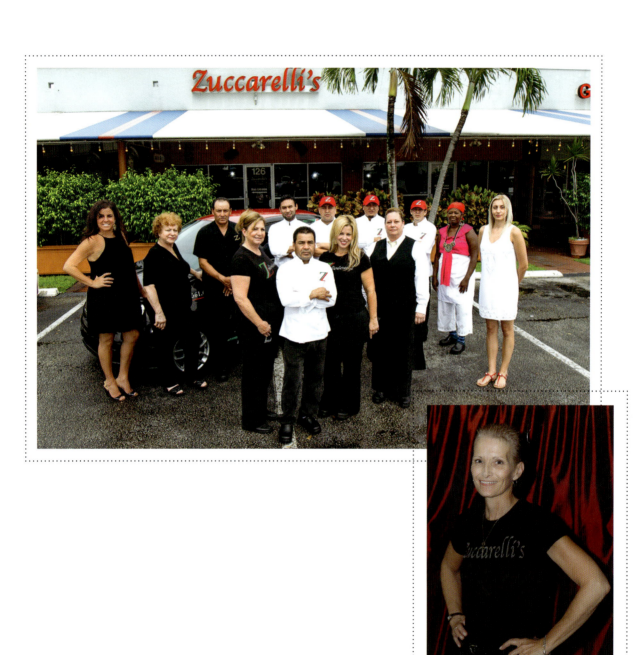

PRAISE FOR ZUCCARELLI'S

Eating at Zuccarelli's is like Sunday dinner at grandma's house. An authentic Italian dinner.

ANTHONY L. MAGLIO, MAGLIO SAUSAGE CO.

Traveling the world has let us enjoy many Italian restaurants but our favorite by far is still and always will be Zuccarelli's! Warm, friendly, and the best Limoncello!

RON AND LESLEE D'AMICO

We found Zuccarelli's over 30 years ago and were hooked…They have something for everyone or will make just what you want, only better than could be imagined…and the tiramisu, make sure to save room! Like a fine wine, Zuccarelli's continues to mature over time…the sophisticated ambience of the dining room or the casual patio makes any occasion extraordinary, and the wine selection ensures complete dining satisfaction! Always greeted warmly, by name, like family, Zuccarelli's feels comfortable like home.

JOHN D. PINSON

Thank you for 20 years of great food and cherished memories with family and friends—We're looking forward to the next 20 years. "Salute."

DAN AND PATRICE PAULONE

If the recipes in your new book are half as good as the food you serve in Zuccarelli's, the book will be a huge success. Wishing you the best from one of your many satisfied customers and a dear friend.

BOB MARCHETTI

Olimpia Zuccarelli has managed to mix savvy chic with her mother's old world Italian recipes to create a unique dining experience. Mangia!

MURIEL AND GENE HOLLAND

We've been coming to Zuccarelli's since its earliest days and in all these years it remains our go-to spot on every occasion, and much more often on no occasion, but just for a great Italian meal! Visiting family members, all of whom have of course joined us there over the years, insist that every visit include at least one trip to "Zucc's" while they're in town!

ARNOLD AND GAIL COHEN

I have been going to Zuccarelli's for 26 years, not only is the food the finest, but you become part of la famiglia.

F. X. CAPRARA

The Zuccarelli's experience is never short of an impeccable one. Delicious, quality food masterfully created by Olimpia. 25 years and we will still stop in twice a week!

JAMES AND DARLENE SPIES

When I am not at home eating my family's recipes at my table I go to Zuccarelli's to enjoy delicious homemade meals at Olimpia's table.

GILDA AND JENNIFER FITZGERALD

I have been a more than satisfied customer of the Zuccarelli restaurant for over 25 years, and I usually frequent it twice a week. Eating there has always been a treat, as the food is excellent and made to order. Olimpia has been like a younger sister to me and I have found her and the restaurant that she so professionally manages to be of the highest quality.

JOE DEDE

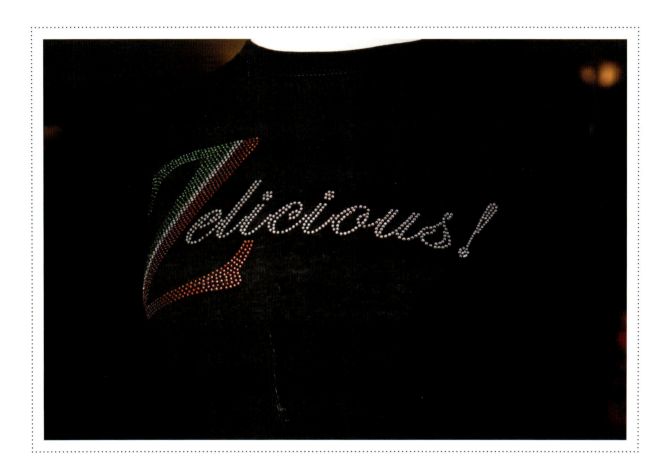

OLIMPIA ZUCCARELLI

FEATURED IN:

Zagat 2013–14

Palm Beach Post 2011–13

Palm Jupiter Magazine

Her Life Magazine

Banzai Magazine

Palm Beach Woman Magazine

PBG Magazine

ABOUT THE AUTHOR

Olimpia Zuccarelli spent her early years in Bronxville, New York, before moving with her family to South Florida in the early 1970s. Her family quickly opened a deli in Pompano Beach, Florida, which later expanded to include the original Zuccarelli's Restaurant. Olimpia's time working in the family restaurant sparked a love for business and cooking that empowered her to expand the family business. Olimpia is now the proud owner and operator of Zuccarelli's Restaurant in West Palm Beach, Florida, where she continues her family's Italian traditions by preparing old world recipes using only the finest ingredients.

Visit www.OlimpiaZuccarelli.com for more information.